The Holy Spirit

Abiding Comforter

"And I will pray the Father, and he shall give you another Comforter, that he may abide with you for ever" (John 14:16).

The Holy Spirit

Abiding Comforter

By
David L. Martin

Rod and Staff Publishers, Inc.
P.O. Box 3, Hwy. 172
Crockett, Kentucky 41413
Telephone (606) 522-4348

Printed in U.S.A

ISBN 978-07399-2326-9

Catalog no. 2474

3   4   5   6   7   —   22   21   20   19   18   17   16   15   14   13

Table of Contents

Preface

Many things have been said about the Holy Spirit, some of them very strange. Maybe it is because people climbed too high (became proud of their understanding) or came too near the brink (stretched their interpretations too far). The Bible warns against the kind of person who insists on "intruding into those things which he hath not seen, vainly puffed up by his fleshly mind" (Colossians 2:18). Perhaps John Bunyan had this kind of person in mind when he wrote the following words:

> Then I saw in my dream, that in the morning the Shepherds called up Christian and Hopeful to walk with them upon the mountains. . . . They had them first to the top of a hill, called Error, which was very steep on the farthest side, and bid them look down to the bottom. So Christian and Hopeful looked down, and saw at the bottom several men dashed all to pieces by a fall that they had from the top. Then said Christian, "What meaneth this?" . . . Then said the Shepherds, "Those that you see lie dashed in pieces at the bottom of this mountain . . . have continued to this day unburied, as you see, for an example to others to take heed how they clamber too high, or how they come too near the brink of this mountain."
>
> —*The Pilgrim's Progress*

Could the same thing happen to us? Yes, very easily, if we fill our minds with knowledge *about* the Holy Spirit but fail to go deep and actually find Him. If the main thing we want is to become experts on this subject and outshine our fellow saints, we are in trouble.

But we can easily avoid this error. Let us remember that the Holy Spirit visits humble places, and look for Him there. Let us seek Him in the company of our brethren, just as the pilgrims stayed in the company of their shepherds. It is right to seek head knowledge—we cannot do without it—but let us seek heart knowledge most of all.

Chapter One

What Is a Spirit?

"A spirit hath not flesh and bones" (Luke 24:39).

God has placed us on this earth to learn both easy and difficult things. He expects us to learn some simple realities through our five senses, but He also expects us to learn that some very real things are beyond physical sensation. In this book, we will "look not at the things which are seen, but at the things which are not seen: for the things which are seen are temporal; but the things which are not seen are eternal" (2 Corinthians 4:18).

Even things that are seen can be hard to define. How do you define the color *green* to a friend who is blind? How then will you explain what a spirit is, when you have never seen one?

We know that our spirit is that which gives us life and the will to live. It gives personality, consciousness, and accountability. But rather than continuing to define the word *spirit,* we might do better to give illustrations.

You are a spirit. You are more than a body. A body could be perfect, as Adam's was when God first made him, and still not be wholly human. It was only when God "breathed into his nostrils the breath of life [that] man became a living soul" (Genesis 2:7). When a person dies, his loved ones weep because the spirit—the real person—is gone.[1] They treat the body with respect because the

---

[1]   We are not making a distinction here between the spirit and the soul.

person once lived in it. But they bury it because his spirit is no longer there.

This does not mean that the body is unimportant. It is a gift from God. But when your body wears out and you "pass away" (quite an accurate way to say it), you will still exist and be conscious. So it is fair to say that you are not so much a body having a spirit, as a spirit having a body.

How different you are from a machine—even a complicated machine! The most complex machines we know are computers. Over the years we have seen them become more and more "intelligent," but that intelligence is artificial. Actually, a computer is no wiser than a lawn mower. It blindly does what it has been programed to do, and there is no consciousness or conscience about it.

The computer that plays chess with the champions does not even know it is playing chess. When it wins a game, its owners may rejoice, but the computer does not. It knows nothing. It might be designed to simulate human personality, but the day it actually has personality is not here and is not even approaching. Machines are machines; spirits are spirits.

Some unfortunate souls have been convinced that people are basically machines—highly complicated machines, of course, so complicated that science has not yet explained all about them— but machines nonetheless. Following that to its logical conclusion, they decide that human aspirations, along with emotions such as love and grief, are mere biological processes in the struggle for survival.

Imagine the predicament of a young man who believes that love has no real meaning and that what feels like love is just the feverish activity of his brain cells! Perhaps the greatest proof that such a theory is wrong is that the people who claim to believe it cannot live as if they believe it. They go on loving, planning, rejoicing, and sorrowing quite as if they were human. As a matter of fact, they are.

Angels are spirits. "Who maketh his angels spirits, and his ministers a flame of fire" (Hebrews 1:7). We can easily understand that because we tend to think of spirits as not being limited by time, space, or gravity. Angels can come and go as they please, and appear or disappear at will.

But angels are no more spirits than we are. They just have more physical freedom. What makes them spirits is the same thing that makes us spirits—they have real intelligence, consciousness, the ability to make choices, accountability for their choices, and so on.

Satan and his demons are spirits. The Bible calls Satan "the spirit that now worketh in the children of disobedience" (Ephesians 2:2). He is not just an influence (like the "Christmas spirit"), for the same verse calls him "the prince of the power of the air."

Furthermore, we know that Satan is a person because the opening chapters of Job record his conversations with God. Again, in Matthew 4 we have the story of how he tempted Christ in person. He has deep feelings, too, as these words from Revelation 12:12 indicate: "The devil is come down unto you, having great wrath, because he knoweth that he hath but a short time." The same could be said for the demons. "The devils also believe, and tremble" (James 2:19).

God is a Spirit. Jesus said those exact words in John 4:24: "God is a Spirit: and they that worship him must worship him in spirit and in truth." This makes it clear that God is alive, that He is aware, that He is wise, that He makes choices. God is a person. His Spirit is more than just an influence: He is the very essence of the all-seeing, all-knowing God.

When speaking of a spirit or even the Holy Spirit, how easily we say "it"! The King James Bible does this too—twice in Romans 8. Verses 16 and 26 both contain the phrase "the Spirit itself." But note what those verses say: the Spirit "beareth witness with our spirit, that we are the children of God," and He "maketh interces-sion for us with groanings which cannot be uttered." Since the Spirit can pray for us better than we can pray for ourselves, He obviously deserves respect as a person in His own right.

Ephesians 4:30 says, "Grieve not the holy Spirit of God." Since we ourselves are spirits who go through joys and sorrows, we eas-ily recognize the personality of the Holy Spirit in this passage.

What is the point of all this? My fellow spirit, when you say "the spirit world," never again think that it is "out there somewhere." A teacher once told her students that there were skeletons in the classroom. The students wondered where those mysterious skele-tons could be until the teacher pointed out that each person in the room had one. Likewise, we live in a spirit world, and every one of us is helping to make it so.

We need to come to grips with our spiritual nature. We cannot deny that we have physical bodies and are compelled to make a physical living. But too many people are content to live, as one observer said, "by their glands and appetites." The apostle Paul said of them, "Whose God is their belly, and whose glory is in their shame, who mind earthly things" (Philippians 3:19). He also said that their end is destruction.

Some people, of course, catch a glimpse of something beyond mere physical existence. That must be the reason Longfellow's "A Psalm of Life" is still popular.

> Tell me not, in mournful numbers,
> "Life is but an empty dream!"
>   .   .   .   .
> Life is real! Life is earnest!
> And the grave is not its goal;
> "Dust thou art, to dust returnest,"
> Was not spoken of the soul.

> Not enjoyment, and not sorrow,
> Is our destined end or way;
> But to act, that each tomorrow
> Find us farther than today.

It is an inspiring poem. But the study of the Holy Spirit runs much deeper and higher than that. Our spirits will not be satisfied with Longfellow's lofty ideals, for we seek fellowship with the Spirit of God. That is why we go to church; that is why we have quiet times with God's Word; that is why we lift our hearts to Him in prayer throughout the day.

Astronomers have discovered that, look where they will in the universe, they can find no demonstrable evidence of intelligent life besides ourselves. They see rocky, barren planets and desolate asteroids, but no one is out there to say hello. Humans appear to be alone in the universe. This prompted the famous remark, "I feel lonely."

Lonely? Not when we discover, like Jacob, that angels of God abound in our desolate places (Genesis 28:11–16). Not when loved ones we have known are waiting for us in realms we have not yet seen. And best of all, not when the Spirit of God is present with us all the time.

> I have Someone to thank for every new day,
> I have Someone to thank for the gifts on life's way,
> He's the One who expects and One who accepts
> All the thanks that I feel each day.
>
> —*Geraldine Koehn*

Chapter Two

What Powers Do Spirits Have?

"The spirit of a man will sustain his infirmity; but a wounded spirit who can bear?" (Proverbs 18:14).

The Bible tells us that Jesus "grew, and waxed strong in spirit" (Luke 2:40). This is no figure of speech. Far from the modern concept of a spirit as a wispy, floating, indefinable essence, there was something within Jesus that gave iron to His being.

What powers do spirits have? We cannot study spirits in a laboratory, but we can go to the Bible and find answers.

Spirits have power over matter. "Let there be—" said God—and there was (Genesis 1:3, 6, 14). This speaks of a Spirit who could command matter into existence. The Bible also tells us that the Lord is "upholding all things by the word of his power" (Hebrews 1:3). Not only did everything come into existence by God's command, everything stays in existence by that same power (2 Peter 3:5–7).

Here we see the spiritual nature of everything that is. By this we are not promoting pantheism, which says everything is God and God is everything. God makes a clear distinction between Himself and the things He has created, and He forbids us to worship any of His creatures. Neither are we promoting animism, which says every object—including a rock or tree—has its own particular spirit. Let us simply observe that God's Spirit is the source of matter and the source of the energy that keeps holding it together.

God showed His power over matter in various ways throughout the Bible. He took off the Egyptians' chariot wheels in the Red Sea. He caught Elijah up to heaven. He gave Samson physical strength that could not be explained in terms of muscles and bones. Delilah herself saw this and said to Samson, "Tell me, I pray thee, wherein thy great strength lieth" (Judges 16:6).

Jesus showed the power of spirit over matter by feeding five thousand with a few loaves and fishes, by walking on the Sea of Galilee, by stilling the wind and waves. In fact, every one of His miracles, from turning water into wine to healing an ear that had been cut off, showed the power of spirit over matter. All these are in addition to His resurrection from death and His ascension into the sky.

Do all spirits have power like that? Thankfully, no. To illustrate the results when God gives evil spirits liberty, note what happened in the first chapter of Job when Satan had a little freedom. Not only did enemies steal animals from Job, but also fire fell from heaven and burned sheep and servants. Further, "there came a great wind from the wilderness" (Job 1:19) and blew down a house, killing all of Job's children. This exception demonstrates the rule that God puts strict limits on evil spirits. May He keep the exceptions few.

By the same token, God has set limits on human spirits. Our spirits alone cannot perform miracles, and we should be thankful that it is so. If everyone could do miracles, this world would be chaos. We do not have the wisdom to control that kind of power.

God assigned your spirit the power to command only your body. That power can seem woefully small. Though some bodies are weak, the spirit does not have any other tool to use. We have no choice about this, as Jesus said, "Which of you by taking thought can add one cubit unto his stature?" (Matthew 6:27). Furthermore, as the body gets older, it hampers the spirit more and more, like the chrysalis of a developing butterfly. The spirit is held inside the body until final release at death.

But every spirit has a certain amount of power, however small.

Sometimes it is amazing how much power a spirit has. In the poem "If—," Rudyard Kipling said,

> If you can force your heart and nerve and sinew
> To serve your turn long after they are gone,
> And so hold on when there is nothing in you
> Except the will which says to them: "Hold on!"

The ability of the human spirit to command the body is powerful enough that God will hold us accountable for it (2 Corinthians 5:10).

Spirits have the power to reason. Here again, look at what God did at Creation. His "Let there be . . ." surely involved not only power but also intelligence. All creation demonstrates God's ability to think. Study the intricacies of an ear with all its inner parts (just an *ear*), and then consider how many other exquisite devices make up a body. Look at the millions of species of plants and animals that God created in only three days; then consider that some tribes of people never even developed the wheel.

God's wisdom resides in His Spirit, not in something physical. A young boy was heard to say, "God's brain must be as big as that house!" He had to be told, "We don't limit God to a brain." There is no end to His intellect.

> There is grace enough for thousands
> Of new worlds as great as this;
> There is room for fresh creations
> In that upper home of bliss.
> —*Frederick William Faber*

But God has limited us to brains for the same reason He has limited us to physical bodies. When we see what human intellect

18

has accomplished, we can guess one reason—not all is well. The horrors of nuclear weapons are just one example. It is safe to say that man needs to prove himself in a limited world before God will give him more freedom.

Spirits have the power to communicate with other spirits. As a rule, your spirit cannot communicate directly with mine, nor mine with yours. Sometimes you meet a person who forgets this. He seems to expect others to catch on to his ideas without his having to express them. His friends wonder what he wants of them and why he is not pleased. He must learn to say what he means, or communicate it by gestures or writing. But most of us consider talking, gesturing, writing, and even paying telephone bills to be well worth the effort. We feel a great urge to communicate with our fellow spirits.

What about other spirits besides human ones—can they communicate with us?

Yes. Unhappily, Satan and his demons can. They too use the five senses to reach the spirits of people. Ask anyone who watches television or who knows much about the World Wide Web. But those are just two of Satan's more notorious methods. Everywhere that people live, Satan tries to transmit his messages by blazing them through the eye gate and by blaring his music and suggestive language through the ear gate.

Besides, Satan has the power to reach people through evil suggestions made directly to their hearts. It seems safe to say that when a godly person unintentionally sees what he should not have seen, an evil spirit often comes to emphasize it and try to make sure it is not forgotten.

Thankfully, good spirits too can communicate with us. The most obvious example is God Himself. He also speaks to us through the five senses. That is one good reason we go to church—to hear what God wants to say to us. "Faith cometh by hearing" (Romans 10:17).

While we sit in church, God also speaks to us directly through His Spirit. He points out things that the preacher or teacher or song-writer may never have thought about, but that are just the things we need to consider. The Spirit underscores the words that are spoken and applies them to our own situation.

Not only can spirits other than humans communicate with us; we can also communicate with them. Some people pray to the devil, and there is no doubt that he gets the message. We have little to say about this subject, for we are to be "wise unto that which is good, and simple concerning evil" (Romans 16:19). How many sinful things have you already learned that you would be happy to forget? Then why learn more? Remember this rule: It is easier to learn than to unlearn, especially about evil.

Studying demonology even from a Christian standpoint can become a snare. The same is true of "talking back to the devil," as some would advocate. We are to "resist the devil" (James 4:7) by the power of God; and often the most effective way to do this is to treat his messages as we would a harassing telephone call: hang up and go about our business.

That brings us to the point of this book: our spirits can communicate and cooperate with a Spirit greater than our own. He is the Holy Spirit of God Himself.[1]

Suddenly our world opens wide. We need not lament the weakness of our spirits. Who needs great power of his own when he can contact the greatest power of all? We need not grieve over our limited intelligence. Who needs a brilliant intellect when all the

---

[1]   Indeed, we not only communicate but we also commune. We not only cooperate but we also share our lives and think the same thoughts. Silas Marner said of his adopted daughter, "We eat of the same bit, and drink of the same cup, and think of the same things from one day's end to the other."

wisdom of God is directing his way?

God has not promised to give us the physical strength of Samson for our tasks, but He has offered us strength from the same source as Samson's. "They that wait upon the LORD shall renew their strength; they shall mount up with wings as eagles; they shall run, and not be weary; and they shall walk, and not faint" (Isaiah 40:31).

God has not promised to make us as wise as Solomon. But consider Jesus' encouragement when He told His disciples that they would be brought before rulers to answer for their faith. He said, "Settle it therefore in your hearts, not to meditate before what ye shall answer: for I will give you a mouth and wisdom, which all your adversaries shall not be able to gainsay nor resist" (Luke 21:14, 15). God can give you more wisdom than your brain can account for. If God could make a donkey talk (Numbers 22:28–30), He can do through you all that He wants.

Many of us are familiar with the saying, "A man is immortal until his work is done," meaning that God will preserve a person's life until he has fulfilled God's purposes for him. Someone has gone a step further and proposed, "A man is invincible until his work is done." That is Biblical, for 2 Corinthians 9:8 says, "And God is able to make all grace abound toward you; that ye, always having all sufficiency in all things, may abound to every good work."

Spirits have the power to choose. The power of choice is in some ways the most awesome power of all. Sometimes it is a minor affair, like choosing dessert at a buffet dinner. But this power can be momentous. We must choose sides in a war—*the* war—the struggle of the ages between God and Satan.

Not that Satan is any match for God; he is no match at all. But God has set things up on earth so that Satan can bid for men's souls on an equal footing with Him. God will not force anyone to join His side. Satan cannot force anyone to join his band either.

Although we have perfect freedom to choose, the odds are against our choosing right. We have a sinful nature that predisposes us to choose wrong. Temptations to sin have a way of coming at the most inconvenient times. Choosing to do right often involves a struggle. "For we wrestle not against flesh and blood, but against principalities, against powers, against the rulers of the darkness of this world, against spiritual wickedness in high places" (Ephesians 6:12).

Even though choosing involves a struggle, it is well worth the struggle. Consider what our options are. The forces of evil compete on even ground with God's forces, but God is immeasurably more powerful than they. Pharaoh's evil magicians, finally beaten, gave this revealing admission: "This is the finger of God" (Exodus 8:19). We hear sometimes of a man who could win a fight with one hand tied behind his back. God can win with one finger.

Jesus illustrated how much more power He had than Satan with these words: "When a strong man armed keepeth his palace, his goods are in peace: but when a stronger than he shall come upon him, and overcome him, he taketh from him all his armour wherein he trusted, and divideth his spoils" (Luke 11:21, 22). Have you ever felt sorry for the strong man who is tied up and has to watch an enemy plunder his palace? Feel sorry no more. That strong man is the devil, and the stronger one is Jesus Christ. Jesus said this to explain how He had power to cast out demons.

Again we see the power of God when Jesus cast an especially strong demon out of a boy. "And the spirit cried, and rent him sore, and came out of him" (Mark 9:26). Observe the frustration of that evil spirit. Like a child forced to give up a toy, he threw the boy down, but he had to give up. He had to come out. Obviously, right and might are ultimately on the same side. So our choice between good and evil should not be hard.

Though the spirits around us are more powerful than we are, they cannot make us toys or pawns in the cosmic struggle. We can choose sides. Only let us remember that once we have chosen, by design or default, we come under the power of the side we have chosen. Satan grips possessively anyone he gets. God also draws people, but with a handclasp rather than with handcuffs. "For it is God which worketh in you both to will and to do of his good pleasure" (Philippians 2:13). The choice is ours. The choice has eternal implications.

> May the pow'rs at my command,
> Soul and body, heart and hand,
> Ever consecrated be;
> May the Christ-life shine in me.
> —*Johnson Oatman, Jr.*

Chapter Three

The Abuse of Spiritual Power

"Thy money perish with thee, because thou hast thought that the gift of God may be purchased with money" (Acts 8:20).

Power is a great thing, but the Bible teaches that it can be a dangerous thing. Laban once told Jacob, "It is in the power of my hand to do you hurt: but the God of your father spake unto me yesternight, saying, Take thou heed . . ." (Genesis 31:29). Even such common things as a box of matches, a wallet full of cash, or a seat behind a steering wheel must be guarded carefully and given only to trusted people. Otherwise, tragic mistakes might be made.

In the case of spiritual power, people can make three mistakes. They can improperly seek contact with God's power. They can make contact with Satan's power. And they can think they made contact with a spiritual power when they made no contact at all. In any of these cases, they might think they are actually finding God.

Improperly seeking contact with God's power. How do people do this? By trying to use God's power for a purpose that God never intended. Simon the sorcerer offered the apostles money for the power to confer the Holy Spirit on people, and for that reason his name is now in the dictionary. Simony is the act of paying money for church offices and religious favors. Peter made it clear to Simon that God's gifts cannot be purchased (Acts 8:18–24).

Seven sons of Sceva in the city of Ephesus made a similar mistake. They undertook to cast out a demon "by Jesus whom Paul preacheth." The demon retorted, "Jesus I know, and Paul I know; but who are ye?" Then he attacked them and chased them out of the house (Acts 19:13–16).

Seeking God's power wrongly may result in a counterfeit. One man walked on water—a supposed miracle—until investigators discovered that he was doing it with the help of stakes whose tops were just beneath the surface. The investigators could have raised a great outcry, but they did not. They simply removed one of the stakes; and at his next performance, the man fell in.

We smile, but was this performer much different from many other people? Some have revival meetings where God's power supposedly produces jumping, shouting, gyrating, and toppling to the floor. Certain ones are even called Holy Rollers because of their excesses. The fact that such power is counterfeit shows up the next day when they continue their life of sin.

Many people—perhaps all of us—have counterfeited the peace and joy that only God can give. Some do it, as one observer said, with "bright smiles and snappy choruses." Some do it by looking calm and self-possessed, even though they know that they are deep in spiritual trouble. God, however, sees through all of this and will expose the façade sooner or later.

There is a sense in which God's power cannot possibly be abused. He simply withholds it from those who would abuse it. But this fact does not stop people from trying, perhaps without even being conscious of it.

Why do people try to abuse God's power? Because they (or we) do not necessarily want to come under God's power; they want God to come under theirs. Perhaps it never occurs to them that He might have a plan that is far better than anything they could command Him to do. He "is able to do exceeding abundantly above all that we ask or think" (Ephesians 3:20).

Making contact with Satan's power. People may do this because they are so desperate for power that they think the powers of darkness are better than nothing. This is astonishing and surely must be born out of ignorance. Who wants to grab an electric fence? Who wants to feed a grizzly bear when signs warn, "The hand that feeds gets eaten"?

The Gadarene demoniac of Mark 5 could have told us, "Don't do it. I've been there, and I most certainly did not enjoy it." Indeed, that man had great power: he could tear chains apart, and no one could confine him. But what a wretched sort of power! It was destructive, and the man lived in torment night and day.

After the demons were cast out of the Gadarene demoniac, he probably felt less power than before. No more could he break chains barehanded. But now he had something much better—the power to live a normal life. No wonder "all men did marvel." Men should marvel even more when someone who has the power to live a normal life wants to dabble in the very thing from which this tormented man was delivered.

Mistakenly thinking that a spiritual power has been contacted. People sometimes credit a spiritual power when they have merely used their own strength and willpower. Astonishing things have been done with human power alone. Books of world records list great feats of willpower and endurance. Perhaps this is what leads people to think that the power within is limitless, maybe even supernatural.

Some people go so far as to make a doctrine out of this. They say that if you visualize something vividly enough and believe in it hard enough, you can make it happen. For example, if they want to persuade someone to do a certain task for them, they picture the person looking interested, then saying, "Sure," and finally getting up and doing the job.

We might as well face it: there is no innate supernatural power in any of us. We simply do not have the ability to make things happen by imagining them, no matter how vividly. The only supernatural powers in the world belong to either Satan or God. If something "impossible" happened, either God did it, Satan did it, or it was no miracle at all.

For people to have faith in their own faith is no innocent matter. It leads them to forget God's plan for their lives while they try to engineer things for themselves. Further, if circumstances do fall into place for them, they tend to give the credit to themselves rather than to God.

All these are reasons why people seek spiritual power and do not find it. God would say to them, "Ye ask, and receive not, because ye ask amiss, that ye may consume it upon your lusts" (James 4:3).

In light of these possible abuses, what does God have in mind for us? Should we not seek spiritual power at all? Of course we should; indeed we must. Powerless Christianity is damnable and empty; it is the reason so many people go looking for power in the wrong places. The Bible describes such religion as "having a form of godliness, but denying the power thereof" (2 Timothy 3:5).

God wants to give the right power in the right amount to the right people. We cannot control the power, but we can let God work in us to make us the right kind of people for the power. In later chapters of this book, we will consider how to be those people.

> Witnessing Thy pow'r to save me,
> Setting free from self and sin;
> Thou who boughtest to possess me,
> In Thy fullness, Lord, come in.
> —*Mary E. Maxwell*

Chapter Four

Who Is the Holy Spirit?

"We have not so much as heard whether there be any Holy Ghost" (Acts 19:2).

"God is a Spirit," Jesus said in John 4:24, and so it follows that the Spirit is—God. This does not mean the Spirit is all there is of God. But it does mean that the Spirit is as truly God as anything else we call God.

The apostle Peter recognized this. He told Ananias, "Why hath Satan filled thine heart to lie to the Holy Ghost? . . . Thou hast not lied unto men, but unto God" (Acts 5:3, 4). Notice that he used *Holy Ghost* and *God* interchangeably. To him, God and the Holy Ghost were the same.

Jesus said, "If a man love me, he will keep my words: and my Father will love him, and we will come unto him, and make our abode with him" (John 14:23). Who is "we"? It is obviously Jesus and the Father because Jesus said so. But just as obviously, the Father will not physically place His throne in our house, neither will Jesus physically walk in the door. Jesus was speaking of what only the Spirit can do. So Father, Son, and Spirit are all united in this verse. The Holy Spirit does not simply represent Father and Son, but is something *of* them. He is one with the Godhead.

How can we become personally acquainted with the Holy Spirit? This is a harder question than how to become acquainted with Jesus. He held children on His lap. He sat down and ate with people. They could easily get to know Him because He was obviously there. But the Spirit? Did He ever touch a leper, tell parables, or let someone anoint His feet?

We can help ourselves considerably if we think of the Holy Spirit as the Spirit of Jesus Christ Himself. (As noted above, He is just as much the Spirit of the Father as of the Son, but the focus here is on the Son.) What Jesus was in flesh, He now is in Spirit.

Jesus said of the Holy Spirit, "Ye know him; for he dwelleth with you, and shall be in you. I will not leave you comfortless: I will come to you" (John 14:17, 18). Who was dwelling with them? That is easy. Jesus was dwelling with the disciples both in body and Spirit. Who would be in them? The Holy Spirit after Pentecost. Jesus brought the two ideas together seamlessly. "He dwelleth with you, and shall be in you." He and His Spirit are one.

Then Jesus added, "I will not leave you comfortless: I will come to you." Earlier Jesus had said "He." Now He said "I." To Him, there was little difference. For all practical purposes, the promised Comforter was Jesus Christ Himself, come in a different form.

When Jesus was baptized, the Spirit descended on Him like a dove. This shows that we can distinguish Spirit from Son. But we cannot separate the two. Jesus was not living without the Spirit up to the time of His baptism. Rather, at the time of baptism, the Spirit took visible form and came on Jesus somewhat like a crown on a man who is already king.

Now we can have a clearer understanding of the Spirit. We can look at Jesus in the Gospels and apply what we see in Jesus' life to the Spirit today. Let us make some observations.

Jesus was a quiet man. "He shall not cry, nor lift up, nor cause his voice to be heard in the street" (Isaiah 42:2). Yes, great crowds followed him, but He often shunned crowds too. He grew up in obscurity, away from public view. Early in His ministry, Jesus "was led by the Spirit into the wilderness" (Luke 4:1). He sought quiet gardens and lonely mountains. He loved small groups of common people and spent much time with them. After doing a miracle, He often said, "Tell no man."

The Spirit of Jesus is quiet too. "He shall not speak of himself," Jesus said in John 16:13. Yes, there was Pentecost, with its "rushing mighty wind," and there have been other great demonstrations of power since then. But the Spirit prefers to work quietly. His favorite work seems to be to live in people's hearts and to make them be like Jesus.

Jesus was interested in people. The multitudes were drawn to Him, partly because they could tell He liked them. Women brought children for His blessing (Mark 10:13, 14). Nicodemus ventured to come to Jesus by night (John 3). Even when Jesus said to a Gentile woman, "It is not meet to take the children's bread, and to cast it unto the dogs," the woman took no offense. She replied, "Yes, Lord: yet the dogs under the table eat of the children's crumbs" (Mark 7:27, 28). There must have been something in His look and tone that kept her coming.

The Spirit of Jesus still loves to dwell among people. "Ye are the temple of the living God; as God hath said, I will dwell in them, and walk in them; and I will be their God, and they shall be my people" (2 Corinthians 6:16). Indeed, He proposes to dwell within our hearts. "What? know ye not that your body is the temple of the Holy Ghost which is in you, which ye have of God, and ye are not your own?" (1 Corinthians 6:19). We marvel at how Jesus condescended to walk in at the doors of ordinary people, sit at their tables, eat their food, and talk their talk. Even more astonishing is His condescension today to move into our hearts and share our little days!

The Spirit of Jesus helps to make us "people persons" too. Naturally some of us are more outgoing, some more retiring. But with the Spirit inside, the outgoing ones will remember to keep people from feeling run over, and the withdrawn ones will in their own quiet way make people feel loved. Today the Spirit of Christ loves people through His people.

Jesus was a man of intercession. To Simon Peter, He said, "I have prayed for thee, that thy faith fail not" (Luke 22:32). When nailed to the cross, He said, "Father, forgive them; for they know not what they do" (Luke 23:34). Even now, "he ever liveth to make intercession" (Hebrews 7:25). What Jesus does, the Spirit also does. "The Spirit itself maketh intercession for us with groanings which cannot be uttered" (Romans 8:26).

Is it any wonder that we feel stirred to pray for our friends and neighbors? and that we are not satisfied until we have prayed for our enemies too, if we have any? Here again, our Lord's Spirit within us moves us to be like Himself.

Jesus "went about doing good" (Acts 10:38). He was no ordinary humanitarian; He acted from the impulse of something alive inside. Today His Spirit stirs us to contribute to the world around us. He helps us to hurt with hurting people and to try to help them, not just through the present crisis, but for their eternal good.

Jesus was zealous. On two occasions He strode into the temple and drove out people and animals. Tables crashed and coins jingled to the floor. "And his disciples remembered that it was written, The zeal of thine house hath eaten me up" (John 2:17). His zeal not only burned hot, it burned long and warm. Zeal kept Him talking to people when He had already talked a long time. Zeal kept Him awake to pray when He had already been awake to pray. Zeal kept Him on the cross hour after bitter hour.

Not surprisingly, today we have people who not only rise to crises but stay steady for the long run. Year after year we find them serving the Lord, never having done enough. They know what it means when they sing, "Oh, may my love to Thee / Pure, warm, and changeless be, / A living fire."[1] The fire is within them, continuing to do what Jesus did on earth.

Jesus was a peacemaker. No one ever traveled farther or worked harder at making things right with people than Jesus did. He traveled from glory to earth, and His efforts took Him to Calvary.

God's children are moved too when things need to be made right between themselves and others. The Lord is stirring them to do so. For them to make an apology or to kindly point out to another person that he is creating a problem is not unnatural.

Jesus was courteous. Shortly after He was crucified, two friends of His walked down the road to Emmaus, talking as they went. A stranger joined them; we know it was Jesus. When they came to their destination, "he made as though he would have gone further" (Luke 24:28). Why so? Because our Lord was and is polite. (He was quite willing to tarry when they said, "Abide with us.") Jesus will not force His way. The word of His Spirit today is, "Behold, I stand at the door, and knock" (Revelation 3:20).

The Guest

He knocks at every door, and forces none.
The choice is yours. There is no latch outside.
Either you leave Him standing there alone,
Or ask Him in to sup with you, and bide.
Either you ask Him in and have Him stay,
Or find your knock unanswered too someday.
—*Margaret Penner Toews*[2]

---

[1] Ray Palmer, "My Faith Looks Up to Thee."
[2] Margaret Penner Toews, *Five Loaves and Two Small Fish* (Neilburg, Saskatchewan: Milton and Margaret Toews, 1976), p. 43. Used by permission.

Chapter Five

How the Holy Spirit Gives Power

"But ye shall receive power, after that the Holy Ghost is come upon you" (Acts 1:8).

Power, as we have already seen, is a great thing in its place, and the Lord expects us to do what it takes to get some of it. We pray, "Give us this day our daily bread" so that we have the physical power to work. We purchase electricity, another form of power, to run our tools and appliances. Then too, we earn money for its power to buy things we need.

There is also mental power—knowledge, for example. We expect a surgeon to have that power when he operates on someone. Our own knowledge we may take for granted, never thinking of it as power—until we forget an important telephone number. Not only knowledge but also the ability to think about what we know is power.

Social power is no small item either. Personal charm and the ability to persuade other people are powers easily abused, but powers nonetheless.

The Lord wants us to have certain physical, mental, and social powers. Most of all, He wants us to have spiritual power. Jesus said, "But ye shall receive power, after that the Holy Ghost is come upon you" (Acts 1:8), and it is perfectly right for us to have some of that power. In fact, the more the better.

Spiritual power can make us like Jesus. With the power of the Holy Spirit, we can overcome temptation as Jesus did. We can reach out and touch our heavenly Father through prayer as Jesus did. We can stand up and be counted for the Lord.

How can we receive the power God wants us to have?

The power of the Holy Spirit in our lives is a bit of a mystery. It is a little like a double-exposed photograph. The first exposure is a picture of us. The second exposure is a picture of Christ, superimposed on our picture.

Consider first the picture of Christ in John 7:37–39: "In the last day, that great day of the feast, Jesus stood and cried, saying, If any man thirst, let him come unto me, and drink. He that believeth on me, as the scripture hath said, out of his belly shall flow rivers of living water. (But this spake he of the Spirit, which they that believe on him should receive: *for the Holy Ghost was not yet given; because that Jesus was not yet glorified.*)" What is the clear implication? That after Jesus was glorified, the Holy Spirit was to be given.

Again, on the day of Pentecost, Peter preached, "This Jesus hath God raised up, whereof we all are witnesses. Therefore being by the right hand of God exalted, and having received of the Father the promise of the Holy Ghost, he hath shed forth this, which ye now see and hear" (Acts 2:32, 33). Instead of the word *glorified,* we have the word *exalted.* The Holy Spirit was given, and is given, when Jesus Christ is glorified . . . exalted . . . honored.

Since the Father had exalted Jesus Christ by the day of Pentecost, why did not everyone in Jerusalem receive the Holy Spirit? Because not only must the Father exalt the Son to provide the Spirit; people too must exalt Him too if they expect to receive the Spirit.

So here again is the fact we have considered before. To receive the Holy Spirit, we receive Jesus Christ. We open our hearts to all that Jesus was in the Gospels and to all that He is in glory, and we find that we are opening our hearts to all that He is on earth in the Spirit. This act superimposes the image of Christ onto our image, making His likeness to be seen in ours.

How can we honor Jesus Christ?

Surrender all control to Him. The issue of control is a real one. Political races, with all their struggle and with all the dollars spent, are about who will control the country. Wars have raged, and families have feuded for years—all over the matter of control. Surrendering control to someone else can be humiliating, even if we are giving it to God. Consequently, many people will not do it.

How did the disciples surrender control to the Lord? They waited patiently in an upper room for the Spirit to come. They let Him come in His own good time. Ten days went by as they humbled themselves and waited.

Shall we also wait for the Holy Spirit? No, because He has already come. Yet we know better than to say there is no waiting involved. Sometimes God postpones His blessing because we are not quite yielding the control of our lives to Him. We might be hurrying off in some direction of our own. We might need to wait for the Lord long enough to realize He is waiting for us—back at the fork in the road! We can honor Him only by retracing our steps and following Him again.

Give all credit to Him. The Acts of the Apostles were in fact the Acts of the Holy Spirit. The apostles were careful to make this clear. When people wanted to worship Paul and Barnabas, these men rent their clothes and begged them to stop. They said, "We also are men" and pointed the people to the living God (Acts 14:11–18).

When we are tempted to take credit for our accomplishments, let us remember the little boy steering a tractor down the farm lane. His feet cannot reach the pedals, and he does not understand the gauges, but he feels important, steering the big tractor. He is sitting on his father's lap, of course.

Honor the Lord's people. We can accomplish some things for the Lord without the company of other saints. There is a saying,

"Lord, help me to remember that nothing will happen today that you and I together can't handle." That flippant request does have some truth, but it leaves out something Jesus said: "Where two or three are gathered together in my name, there am I in the midst of them" (Matthew 18:20).

The Bible also says that with the Lord's power, one person would "chase a thousand, and two put ten thousand to flight" (Deuteronomy 32:30). Notice the development. One person chases one thousand; two chase not two thousand but ten thousand. Not only the individual but also the group is precious to the Lord, and we honor Him by giving the group its due honor.

Appreciate the power He has already given you. What do you do when you serve a little child at the supper table and he cries because you did not give him more? Probably you say, "Eat what you have, and then we'll see about more."

All of us who belong to the Lord have *some* of the Spirit's power. Do we appreciate and use what we do have? Why ask for more power when we have not even thanked the Lord for the power He has given?

Often we are too farsighted. We say that God "is able to do exceeding abundantly above all that we ask or think" (Ephesians 3:20), and we imagine some great blessing away out there. How many possibilities for service has He placed right in front of us? It is a great blessing to be able to pick up the telephone or write a letter to encourage a friend a thousand miles away. Maybe the Lord has placed that or some other power for service at your door. Whatever it is, take it up and thank the Lord for it.

Appreciate what the Spirit has done for you through others. You do not always have to be giving. Sometimes you must be the recipient. Yes, "it is more blessed to give than to receive" (Acts 20:35); but sometimes other people need that blessing too—the blessing of giving. Do you value what they have done for you?

Consider all that has already been given us by way of the printed page. We should not take it for granted; millions in the past either could not read or had little to read. Today our churches have schools to teach us how to read and publishing houses to provide an abundance of reading material. Do we find time to read at least some of it?

On top of all this is the gift of Jesus Christ Himself, who lived with us and died for us to provide our redemption. "Thanks be unto God for his unspeakable gift" (2 Corinthians 9:15).

Think again of our double exposure with Christ. The longer we allow the power of His Spirit to dwell in us, the clearer His image becomes. And our image fades.

John the Baptist understood this. He was a man under the power of the Holy Spirit. Crowds came to hear him preach. Yet when speaking of Jesus, John said, "He must increase, but I must decrease" (John 3:30).

Interestingly, crowds did not come to hear John all his life. He spent his last days in a squalid prison cell and died at a relatively young age. Did that mean John had lost the Spirit's power? No. It just meant that the Spirit had a different task for him to do.

The apostle Paul also understood this truth. He wrote, "I was with you in weakness, and in fear, and in much trembling. And my speech and my preaching was not with enticing words of man's wisdom, but in demonstration of the Spirit and of power" (1 Corinthians 2:3, 4). Where did the power come from? Obviously not from Paul, for he was suffering weakness, fear, and trembling.

Paul emphasized this again in his second letter to the same people. "But we have this treasure in earthen vessels, that the excellency of the power may be of God, and not of us" (2 Corinthians 4:7).

How can we decrease so that God's power can work?

Accept personal humiliations. Paul wrote, "And lest I should be exalted above measure through the abundance of the revelations, there was given to me a thorn in the flesh, the messenger of Satan to buffet me, lest I should be exalted above measure. For this thing I besought the Lord thrice, that it might depart from me. And he said unto me, My grace is sufficient for thee: for my strength is made perfect in weakness. Most gladly therefore will I rather glory in my infirmities, that the power of Christ may rest upon me. . . . When I am weak, then am I strong" (2 Corinthians 12:7–10).

One reason it usually takes a long time to write a book may be that people would take too much credit to themselves if it came too easily. By the time all the difficulties and inefficiencies are over and the writer's self-image has crumbled, the book is born. You can add illustrations from your own experience.

Let go of personal power. Personal power can hinder what the Spirit is trying to do. A woman who takes fingerprints said one of her biggest problems is having people understand that they should not try to help her. All they need to do is cooperate and let her roll their fingers on the paper. Great personal energy is fine in its place. It can sell a car or a pair of shoes, but it cannot win a soul for the Lord or give the Lord the kind of service He wants.

Fill the place marked out for you. Are you sure the Lord wants you to be a great evangelist? There is no point in asking God to empower you for things He does not want you to do. Electricity will not empower a kitchen blender to sweep the floor, no matter how much power is available. Fasting forty days and forty nights in a wilderness will not make you another Jesus Christ. Going to Africa and tramping around will not make you a successful missionary. No matter how good a Christian you are, filling the place

38

God has for you is the only way to please Him. He will give you all the power you need to fill that place.

Let Jesus work quietly within. We tend to be childish. We like high drama. We would rather command stones to become bread than quietly suffer hunger. We would rather walk on water than pray all night. We would rather come down from a cross than remain nailed to it. How different by nature we are from Jesus Christ, who loved to do the quiet little things!

The tract *Others May, You Cannot* makes these observations: "The Lord may let others be honored and put forward, and keep you hidden in obscurity, because He wants to produce some choice, fragrant fruit for His coming glory, which can be produced only in the shade. He may let others be great, but keep you small. He may let others do work for Him and get the credit for it, but He will make you work and toil without knowing how much you are doing. And then to make your work still more precious, He may let others get the credit for the work you have done, making your reward ten times greater when Jesus comes."

In summary, the path to power is to stop wanting it for yourself and start wanting it for the Lord. Are you afraid by this time even to ask for it? Fear no longer. Jesus said, "Whatsoever ye shall ask in my name, that will I do, that the Father may be glorified in the Son" (John 14:13). He is far from being offended by our asking. Rather, He is glorified. For if we ask something for ourselves in His Name, we are asking it for Him.

> Let my hands perform His bidding,
> Let my feet run in His ways,
> Let my eyes see Jesus only,
> Let my lips speak forth His praise.
> —Mary D. James

Chapter Six

The Holy Spirit
Among the Brotherhood

"There is one body, and one Spirit, . . . one Lord, one faith, one baptism" (Ephesians 4:4, 5).

The idea that the Holy Spirit works through groups of believers has been neglected in many churches. Too many church members feel free to do whatever they please and to call it the leading of the Spirit. They feel answerable only to their own judgment rather than to the church group.

No doubt, the mentality of the world around us has helped to bring this thinking into the church. In our society, the individual stands tall. The word *collective* reminds people of communism with its collective farms and factories—not an attractive way of life to most of us.

But as usual, we can find a balance in the Bible. On the day of Pentecost, how did the Spirit manifest Himself? For one thing, tongues as of fire rested on each of the disciples present (Acts 2:3). That spoke of the Holy Spirit's dwelling in each individual. But the believers also heard the sound of a rushing mighty wind. That was an experience they all shared together.

They spoke in various tongues; the Spirit was working in each individual. But they all preached the same Gospel; the Spirit was working through the group. No one hoarded or monopolized the Holy Spirit.

Other New Testament passages bring out the same balance. "What? know ye not that your body is the temple of the Holy Ghost which is in you, which ye have of God, and ye are not your own?" (1 Corinthians 6:19). That speaks of God dwelling in the hearts of individuals. But note another verse: "Know ye not that ye are the temple of God, and that the Spirit of God dwelleth in you?" (1 Corinthians 3:16). Here the language is a little different. *(Ye* is an archaic plural pronoun.) Here God is dwelling among the believers collectively.

Ephesians 2:21, 22 makes it even more plain. This passage speaks of "an holy temple in the Lord: in whom ye also are builded together for an habitation of God through the Spirit." Believers in the church are like stones making up the walls of the temple where God makes His home.

What does the Spirit do for the group?

He provides a common standing. Notice how quickly people become friendly to each other when they find that they share a common memory (the same school or community), a common experience (heart surgery), or a common interest (motherhood). The Holy Spirit gives people something precious to draw them together. "For by one Spirit are we all baptized into one body, whether we be Jews or Gentiles, whether we be bond or free; and have been all made to drink into one Spirit" (1 Corinthians 12:13).

He honors the prayers of the group. If the Holy Spirit ever honored the prayers of one man, it seems it would have been the apostle Paul's. Certainly Paul did pray alone, but he also entreated his fellow believers, "Strive together with me in your prayers to God for me" (Romans 15:30). His words to the Ephesians also reveal how he treasured the prayers of the group: "Praying always with all prayer and supplication in the Spirit, and watching thereunto with all perseverance and supplication for all saints; *and for me*" (Ephesians 6:18, 19).

Christians often get together to pray, as they did when Peter was in prison (Acts 12:12). But after parting, they can still pray together through the same Spirit.

He calls church leaders. "The Holy Ghost hath made you overseers," said Paul to the elders of Ephesus (Acts 20:28). In other words, He oversees the overseers. Paul knew firsthand what he was talking about, as we see in Acts 13:2. "As they ministered to the Lord, and fasted, the Holy Ghost said, Separate me Barnabas and [Paul] for the work whereunto I have called them."

He directs in church decisions. After Jesus told His disciples, "I have yet many things to say unto you, but ye cannot bear them now," He added, "Howbeit when he, the Spirit of truth, is come, he will guide you into all truth" (John 16:12, 13). Some students of history say that Jesus gave insufficient direction to His followers for the founding of a religion—how to organize a church, for example. Rather, Jesus saw that the disciples could not handle everything at the moment. He intended that the Spirit would direct those matters later.

And so it was. As the Church Age began, some Christians were not sure how to make the transition from Old Testament to New Testament practices. How fast and how far should they go? To help decide this, many leaders gathered for the Jerusalem conference. Someone else came who was not listed on the roster—the Holy Spirit. There was much debate, but finally the discussion fell in line with what the Spirit wanted. The church leaders were confident of this; for when they drew up their final decision, they wrote, "It seemed good to the Holy Ghost, and to us" (Acts 15:28).

He helps us to draw lines for our own times. There are questions the New Testament does not specifically address, such as the use of modern inventions, the use of tobacco, the matter of television, and the proper way to dress in the twenty-first century. We find principles that apply to these issues in the New Testament, but no specific applications.

One religious group has the following creed: "Where the Scriptures speak, we speak; where the Scriptures are silent, we are silent." That sounds good, but one may guess that it leaves many practical questions unanswered. Here is where the Spirit comes in. Not everyone who follows the Spirit will end up making his clothes after the exact same pattern. But all who follow the Spirit will make applications that fit the principles outlined in the Scriptures.

What are some wrong ideas about the Spirit's work with the group?

Error: *Since we all have the Holy Spirit, my word is as good as yours.* Miriam and Aaron dared to criticize Moses sharply, defending their attitude by saying, "Hath the LORD indeed spoken only by Moses? hath he not spoken also by us?" (Numbers 12:2). The Bible adds, "And the LORD heard it"—suddenly putting the whole episode into a new perspective. The offenders were punished. True, God's Spirit is for everyone, but the Spirit has not given everyone the same gifts and insights or the same authority. Moses obviously had a greater gift of stable leadership than Aaron or Miriam did, and God had placed Moses as leader over them. They should have respected that.

It is interesting that Moses' father-in-law once took him aside and said, "The thing that thou doest is not good" (Exodus 18:17) and gave him some fatherly advice. But he did it as a father-in-law and onlooker. He did not challenge the wisdom Moses had. Rather, he built on it.

Error: *Since the Spirit dwells among the group, leaders have no particular authority.* Korah, Dathan, and Abiram defied Moses and Aaron with these words: "Ye take too much upon you, seeing all the congregation are holy, every one of them, and the LORD is among them: wherefore then lift ye up yourselves above the congregation of the LORD?" (Numbers 16:3). Strangely, the rebels were leaders themselves. By saying this, they were undercutting their own authority.

To have a church, we must respect the various offices of the church. If we choose a song leader, we must follow him. If he has trouble with a song, some people in the audience might help him start it right. But he is still the song leader, and we respect him as such. The same principle applies to any other kind of church leader.

Error: *All unity in the church is unity of the Spirit.* We should see the fallacy of this statement just by looking at it. But it is an easy error to fall into, simply because unity feels so good! However, the spirit of unity is not necessarily the unity of the Spirit that Ephesians 4:3 speaks of. Just feeling cozy together is not enough. Our unity must be based on the Holy Spirit's directions; and these directions, of course, are found in the Bible.

Error: *The church is a democracy.* In some ways, the church resembles a democracy because it values the voice of every member. Most church groups do a certain amount of voting, which is one of the marks of a democracy. Yet the difference between the church and a democracy is profound. A democracy is "of the people, by the people, for the people." It is answerable to the people, and the people have the last word.

The church is a theocracy (government by God), answerable to the Lord Himself. "For of him, and through him, and to him, are all things" (Romans 11:36). Even though we draw upon the viewpoints of many members, each member must keep his heart in tune with God.

Error: *I can be just as spiritual outside the group as in it.* Even assuming that you are filled with the Spirit, how long will you remain so if you distance yourself from other Spirit-filled people? A burning coal placed a distance away from the fireplace might burn for a time as brightly as any coal in the fireplace, but before long it will cool off and go out. Burning coals need not only the fire within themselves but also the fire in each other. And so do we.

A common factor in most of these wrong ideas is the lack of submission. Such a spirit is just the opposite of the general New Testament tone, with its emphasis on surrender to God and submission to fellow believers. The true Christian spirit is probably best summarized in Peter's words: "Yea, all of you be subject one to another, and be clothed with humility: for God resisteth the proud, and giveth grace to the humble" (1 Peter 5:5).

> Not alone we conquer,
>   Not alone we fall;
> In each loss or triumph
>   Lose or triumph all.
> Bound by God's far purpose
>   In one living whole,
> Move we on together
>   To the shining goal!
>   —*Frederick L. Hosmer*

Chapter Seven

Praying in the Holy Ghost

"But ye, beloved, building up yourselves on your most holy faith, praying in the Holy Ghost, keep yourselves in the love of God" (Jude 20, 21).

Prayer is a thing of the spirit. No copper telephone lines link us to God. Neither can we explain prayer in terms of radio waves. Yet we confidently call upon God, and He hears and answers.

Actually, prayer is a thing of two spirits—our own and God's. Neither spirit alone can make a complete connection. There has to be active transmission on our part and active reception on the Lord's.

We need not worry that the Lord's receiver will fail to work. But many prayers fail because they are not transmitted right. Always the problem can be summed up in one word: sin. Two sins in particular will hinder prayer.

The sin of a lazy spirit. Prayer and electronic communication have one thing in common: they both take energy. When you speak on the telephone, your voice causes a very tiny disturbance in a very weak electrical current. Those little impulses then enter the telecommunications system and are boosted as far across the country as you like. The real power is in the system, not in you.

But there is one thing you must do that the system will not do for you. You must talk! When you are talking to someone very important to you, you put all your energy into your talking. This does not mean that you speak loudly, but you do your very best to get your ideas across.

Such is prayer. Paul wrote to the Colossians that Epaphras was "always *labouring fervently* for you in prayers" (Colossians 4:12). Paul besought the Romans to "*strive* together with me in your prayers to God" (Romans 15:30). When Peter was put in prison, "prayer was made *without ceasing* of the church unto God for him" (Acts 12:5).

Laziness ruins prayer. Our prayer will hardly qualify as a prayer if we rise from our knees barely knowing what we prayed for. We can hardly expect an impulse from our spirits to reach the heart of God if it did not even stir our own hearts.

Some of us by nature will need to go through a greater struggle against laziness in order to pray effectively. Then let us struggle. One thing we can do is not make ourselves too comfortable while praying. The Christian who sinks by the side of his bed at 10:00 P.M. to pray, knees on a soft rug, head in a warm nest, will probably not pray very well. After wakening at 1:00 A.M. a time or two, still on his knees, he should take the hint and pray in some other time and way.

Another thing we can do is collect our thoughts. One Christian had much trouble along this line until he began to commit his thoughts to paper. He numbered each person or item he prayed about and wrote the initial of that person or item. At the close of his prayer period, he had something to show for his time. It was a dot-to-dot way of praying, but it was certainly better than dreaming the time away.

George Mueller used the Bible as his guide for praying. After asking the Lord's blessing, he would begin to read. Soon he would come to a verse that reminded him of something he wanted to pray about. He would pray for a friend, offer thanksgiving, or confess a wrong. Then he would read on.

If your mind goes off track after you have been kneeling awhile, get up for a time. Sit, stand, or pace the floor. If you have trouble keeping track of your prayers when you only think them, whisper them. Do what works; but whatever you do, pray.

Sometimes people become lazy in prayer because they have slipped into a routine. (A routine is good to a point; a better word might be *rut*.) Have you gotten to the point where you can pray the same prayers without thinking about what you are praying? Commit your problem to the Lord. God has ways of getting people out of ruts. He knows that a little desperation does not hurt us. So go ahead. Get desperate. You might discover that God will use your desperation to solve your problem.

Here is a simple way to stay out of such a rut. If you have items you regularly mention in prayer, pray about them in a different order on different days. Do whatever helps to keep you aware that you are praying and that God is listening with interest.

Someone summed it up this way: "Pray earnestly; don't expect a thousand-dollar answer to a ten-cent prayer."

The sin of an activist spirit. When we pray, we must recognize that most of the activity takes place on the Lord's end. Jesus "ever liveth to make intercession for [us]" (Hebrews 7:25). "Likewise the Spirit also helpeth our infirmities: for we know not what we should pray for as we ought: but the Spirit itself maketh intercession for us with groanings which cannot be uttered" (Romans 8:26). God is no passive receiver. He has appointed Son and Spirit not only to amplify our prayers but to put them into His own language.

How then should we pray? We read in Ephesians 2:18, "For through [Christ] we both have access by one *Spirit* unto the Father." Likewise we read in that beloved passage about the Christian's armor, "Praying always"—how? "With all prayer and supplication *in the Spirit*" (Ephesians 6:18).

The prophets of Baal leaped around their altar on Mount Carmel as they tried to call fire from heaven (1 Kings 18:25–29). They prayed with great intensity of spirit, but they were not praying in the Spirit. (They were not even praying to the right God.) Could it be that we too might pray spirited prayers without praying in the Spirit?

At first this might seem impossible, since our God, after all, is there. How could He who knows everything fail to hear? Because He who knows everything might recognize that we are praying in our own energy and failing to come to Him in the way He has ordained. We could be praying in the name of our own fervency or even in the name of our own noise. (A Christian woman, after attending a service where some loud prayers were offered, said wryly, "I'm afraid my prayers don't get very far!")

In whose name shall we pray? Jesus said, "And whatsoever ye shall ask in my name, that will I do, that the Father may be glorified in the Son. If ye shall ask any thing in my name, I will do it" (John 14:13, 14). "Ye have not chosen me, but I have chosen you . . . that whatsoever ye shall ask of the Father in my name, he may give it you" (John 15:16). "Verily, verily, I say unto you, Whatsoever ye shall ask the Father in my name, he will give it you. Hitherto have ye asked nothing in my name: ask, and ye shall receive, that your joy may be full" (John 16:23, 24).

This does not mean that we should merely append the words "in Jesus' Name" to our prayers, even though this is a good practice. Rather, we should understand that only through Jesus do our prayers have any hope of reaching the throne of God, and pray in that spirit.

Note Jesus' description of the right way to pray. "When thou prayest, enter into thy closet, and when thou hast shut thy door, pray to thy Father which is in secret" (Matthew 6:6). This is a calm, quiet approach that expects very little of its own prayers but everything of God.

Sometimes people become unhappy if others do not understand them when they talk. Finally they overdo it and speak very loudly and plainly indeed. We might find ourselves doing something similar when the Lord does not seem to be hearing. Realizing at this point that we are praying wrong leads us to wonder if our prayers were defective all along. Maybe we were depending on our energy in prayer to get results, rather than depending on God.

Fervency in prayer can actually show a right spirit. "The effectual fervent prayer of a righteous man availeth much" (James 5:16). God must like to see it, as we like to see our children fervent in whatever they are doing. But the thing that brings our prayers before the throne is the fervency of the Lord's Spirit rather than the fervency of our spirit. The most heartfelt prayer still needs the Spirit's intercession. If we recognize this, we will be doing what Jude 20 says: "praying in the Holy Ghost."

> Nothing in my hands I bring,
> Simply to Thy cross I cling.[1]

---

[1] Augustus M. Toplady, "Rock of Ages."

Chapter Eight

The Holy Spirit in Testifying

"And he gave some, . . . evangelists" (Ephesians 4:11).

It must have looked like a huge assignment when Jesus told His little band, "Ye shall be witnesses unto me both in Jerusalem, and in all Judaea, and in Samaria, and unto the uttermost part of the earth" (Acts 1:8). Naturally the disciples knew that more and more believers would join them and make the work more possible. More importantly, they had the comfort of knowing that they would be working along with the Holy Spirit. The entire responsibility for the task would not fall on their shoulders.

Yet some responsibility would be theirs. Like a father giving tasks to his children, God gave tasks to them and allowed His Spirit to be helped or hindered by their performance of the work. He does the same today. There are several basic lessons we should learn.

We can help the work of the Spirit as individuals. The Lord works through different people in different ways. A man might hand out tracts on a college campus. A young woman might take part with a church group in a street meeting. A teenage boy or girl might recite some memorized verses or help to sing in a cottage meeting, or befriend the son or daughter of a family visiting church. An elderly lady might call a struggling sister on the telephone to encourage her.

This is the way it was at the very beginning of church life. In

Acts 13:2, "the Holy Ghost said, Separate me Barnabas and Saul for the work whereunto I have called them." Barnabas and Saul (Paul) had a work separate from that of the other people, even though they all came under the direction of the same Spirit. These two went on a missionary trip; the rest stayed home. This does not mean that those who stayed home did nothing, but obviously they did not travel as Paul did.

The Spirit not only works in different ways with different people, but He also works in different ways with the same people at different stages of life. Sometimes He calls us to be more active, sometimes to be more quiet. Paul and Barnabas came home from their missionary journey, "and there they abode long time with the disciples" (Acts 14:28). Again, this does not mean they did nothing; they simply served the Lord in a different capacity than they did before.

We can become too rigid in this matter of testifying. We can too easily picture doing it in a way we saw someone else do it or in a way someone did it in a missionary book we read. If our method does not follow the same pattern, we might suppose we are not doing it right. In the process, we might be overlooking certain things that the Lord has in mind just for us.

> True worth is in *being*, not *seeming*,
> In doing, each day that goes by,
> Some little good—not in dreaming
> Of great things to do by and by.
> —*Alice Cary*

Now let us go back to the story of Paul and Barnabas for our second major point.

We can help the work of the Spirit as a group. We observed that the Spirit called Paul and Barnabas to do something different from what other people were doing. But at the same time, He did not call them to divorce themselves from everyone else. Their mission effort was actually a team effort. Men at home fasted, prayed, laid hands on them, and commissioned them to go. The ones at home prayed for them (we may safely assume) while they were away. When the missionaries came home, they called the church together and "rehearsed all that God had done with them" (Acts 14:27).

Team effort applies especially to prayer. Great revivalists, though men of prayer themselves, depended much on prayer warriors whose names we have never heard. Look again at the "upper room" experience. How many people were there? One hundred twenty (Acts 1:15). They all prayed together and all shared together in the consummation when the Holy Spirit came. Yet we know the names of only a few. Many unnamed souls contributed their prayers before the event came to pass.

Team effort applies also to personal example. Evangelists, of course, should show by their lives what the Christian faith is all about. Yet they depend on many examples besides their own. This might be a new thought to some of us. It is not only our own testimony that we make or break by our example. We help or harm other people's testimonies too.

In fact, we can help or harm the cause of God Himself. This brings us to our third point.

We can hinder the work of the Spirit. The Holy Spirit will not do our work for us. This can be a frightening thought. Suddenly we realize that the burden of our work is on us rather than on the Spirit. Our success as soul winners does not depend on our persuading the Spirit to speak. He will speak, but He wants *us* to speak in cooperation with Him.

The apostle Paul must have sensed this. He said to the Ephesians, "[Pray] for me, that utterance may be given unto me, that I may open my mouth boldly, to make known the mystery of the gospel" (Ephesians 6:19). He realized that since "faith cometh by hearing" (Romans 10:17), it was his business to make the Gospel heard. Then the Spirit could continue the work.

In the matter of testifying, there is good reason to suspect that we do not run ahead of the Lord nearly as often as we run behind. It seems so much easier for a typical housewife to make another dish of graham cracker fluff than to make a simple phone call to the community lady who came to church last Sunday. It seems much more natural for a girl to sew another dress than to take some home-made bread across the street to the old neighbor man sitting on his front porch, and maybe even to ask him if he loves the Lord. It seems more businesslike for the man in public life to keep his schedule marching than to take time out for the customer who needs to talk.

How can we help the Holy Spirit rather than hinder Him?

Go through the doors already open. Where there are great evidences of the Spirit's blessing, you always find people who had already been busy serving the Lord. Help hand out papers when asked to do so. Give your testimony when it is called for. Quote the assigned memory verse. Help to sing!

Nudge some doors if you think they will open. If you have been carrying tracts around, wondering who to give them to, start with a cashier if he or she is not too busy at the moment. Say, "Here's a little inspiration for you today." If the person hesitates, you might add, "I love the Lord, and I like to say a good word for Him sometimes." Some will say, "Sure" and take it. Others will say, "No, thanks." But do it anyway.

Do the obvious things first. You have perhaps read about great revivals kindled by people who prayed hour after hour as if it were a part-time job. Some of them prayed half the night. I am not saying that is the only way to get results. But let me ask you this: When a week of revivals is held at your church and pre-service prayer meetings are announced, do you go?

Finally, "quench not the Spirit" (1 Thessalonians 5:19). Deliberately putting a damper on the inner fire of urgency has much to do with lack of success in testifying. Certainly we should use a gentle and courteous approach in speaking to people; the Holy Spirit does. But we should also be willing to risk being rebuffed; the Holy Spirit does that too.

Remember, each person we meet is headed for glory or despair. Either he will hear his name pronounced by Jesus before the angels (Revelation 3:5), or he will hear "Depart from me, ye cursed, into everlasting fire" (Matthew 25:41). Not many people believe this anymore, but you believe it, I believe it, and the Holy Spirit believes it. Does He have something in mind for you to do about it today?

> There was a man who prayed for wisdom that he might
> Sway men from sinful ways and lead them into light.
> Each night he knelt and asked the Lord
> To let him guide the sinful horde.
> And every day he rose again to idly drift along,
> One of the many common men who form the common
>   throng.[1]

---

[1] *Poems With Power to Strengthen the Soul,* c. 1907.

Chapter Nine

The Holy Spirit in Victory Over Sin

"We wrestle . . . against spiritual wickedness in high places" (Ephesians 6:12).

What could be more critically important than victory over sin? Victory is a visible way of measuring our relationship with the Lord. If we cannot claim victory that we have seen, how can we claim forgiveness that we have not seen? If the present is not settled, how can we be sure that "the old account was settled long ago"? But if we do have victory over sin, that bolsters our assurance that all is well between us and the Lord. "Beloved, if our heart condemn us not, then have we confidence toward God" (1 John 3:21).

Victory over sin gives us a credible testimony, one that people believe. Either you are a good person or you are not; even sinners know the difference. If they recognize that you are a good person, they might not agree with what you say; but at least they will know that you believe it and live it. That is no small matter.

Victory over sin makes the difference between the road to heaven and the road to hell. A person who habitually sins is a sinner; we might as well face that fact. One who habitually avoids sin is a saint on the way to glory. "Little children, let no man deceive you: he that doeth righteousness is righteous. . . . He that committeth sin is of the devil" (1 John 3:7, 8).

To find victory over sin, we must cooperate with the Holy Spirit. It is very important that we let the Spirit do for us what we cannot do for ourselves. A child learning to ride a bicycle has to learn a similar lesson. At first he is more concerned about not falling than about going anywhere. He tries to balance himself, which is of course impossible for him to do by his own efforts. After he learns to "quit trying and start trusting," his troubles are over. As he moves forward, the gyroscopic forces of the whirling wheels help to hold him up. We will look first at what the Spirit does for us in giving us victory over sin, and then at certain things He expects us to do.

What does the Holy Spirit do?

He transforms us. An ungodly man was converted and later met one of his former buddies on the street. Knowing the evil in the other man's heart, he passed on without greeting him. His former friend called after him, "It's me!" The Christian called back, "Yes, but it's not me!" Once the Spirit gives us a new life, we have new interests and no longer pay attention when temptation crooks its finger. Without this transformation, no strategy we employ to keep from sinning will be of any lasting value.

He stands present with us. When someone we respect stands nearby, we become more mindful of our behavior. We might wish that the Lord were physically present so that we would find it easier to overcome temptation. Very well. He is present in Spirit, and remembering this will make it easier to do right. David Livingstone wrote that during his adventures and dangers in Africa, he was sustained by one promise in particular: "Lo, I am with you alway, even unto the end of the world" (Matthew 28:20). As we travel through territory just as dangerous—infested not by scorpions and fevers but by demons and temptations—that promise is still true.

He shields us from spiritual dangers we did not know existed. "And he shewed me Joshua the high priest standing before the angel of the LORD, and Satan standing at his right hand to resist him. And the LORD said unto Satan, The LORD rebuke thee, O Satan; even the LORD that hath chosen Jerusalem rebuke thee: is not this a brand plucked out of the fire?" (Zechariah 3:1, 2). Did Joshua know about this conflict in the spirit world? Probably not.

In our spiritual contest, the Lord moderates temptations for us. Satan complained to God about Job, "Hast not thou made an hedge about him, and about his house, and about all that he hath on every side?" (Job 1:10). It is not certain that Job knew about the hedge, but there was one, and God kept it there (although He adjusted it for His own purposes).

By the same token, "there hath no temptation taken you but such as is common to man: but God is faithful, who will not suffer you to be tempted above that ye are able; but will with the temptation also make a way to escape, that ye may be able to bear it" (1 Corinthians 10:13).

He forbids us to do all we feel like doing. Humans can think up all kinds of evil without help from the devil. People sometimes say, "The devil made me do it!" Not necessarily. "Every man is tempted, when he is drawn away of *his own lust,* and enticed" (James 1:14). The result is a conflict between what a Christian wants and what the Spirit wants, and the Spirit will not back down. "The flesh lusteth against the Spirit, and the Spirit against the flesh: and these are contrary the one to the other: so that ye cannot do the things that ye would" (Galatians 5:17).

Notice that "ye cannot." The Spirit, like a good parent, sometimes says no. And He means it.

He gives us a sword. "Take . . . the sword of the Spirit, which is the word of God" (Ephesians 6:17). The Spirit has already spoken through the printed page. We must now become familiar with the Word so we can avail ourselves of the right Scripture verse when we need it. This means memorizing key portions of the Bible.

"Thy word have I hid in mine heart, that I might not sin against thee" (Psalm 119:11).

Perhaps the verse we need in the moment of temptation is a simple prohibition like "Thou shalt not covet." However, the most effective verse may be one that helps you look away from the temptation. One of this writer's favorite victory verses is "Thou wilt shew me the path of life: in thy presence is fulness of joy; at thy right hand there are pleasures for evermore" (Psalm 16:11). Another excellent one is "No good thing will he withhold from them that walk uprightly" (Psalm 84:11).

In other words, no one needs to feel cheated out of something special because he resisted temptation! The glories of the world to come far exceed anything we give up in order to live a godly life. In fact, the marvel of having the Lord in this life is already better to us than our sins. Anyone who knows how to use the sword of the Spirit will understand these things.

He corrects us if we sin or fail. According to one saying, "Your best friend won't tell you" that your face is dirty or that you smell like the last place you visited. Actually, your closest friend—a husband or wife or brother or sister—*will* tell you. Best friends desire that openness.

The Spirit will say, not in so many words but deep in the heart, "Yes, that little incident was amusing, but don't keep running it through your mind again and again. Be an adult, and move on." Or "You brushed your friend off too quickly. How would you have felt in his place?" Or "Why did you laugh like that?" Or "You condemn yourself too much, as if your mistakes prove that you are a failure. They don't, you know."

By rebuking us for little offenses, the Holy Spirit steers us away from big ones. We might feel frustrated by our sensitivity and wonder why our conscience cannot be more free like someone else's. Of course, there is such a thing as an overly sensitive conscience.

On the other hand, the person whom we envy might not feel any more free in conscience than we do. We concern ourselves about little offenses; would we rather have bigger ones to worry about?

What must we do?

We have considered what the Spirit does for us. Now, how do we cooperate with the Spirit in winning victory over sin? Is there a part for us to play? Yes, we must do what we can, and God will do what we cannot. A child on a bicycle has to pedal and observe safety rules. Not everything will be done for him. In the book *God Is for the Alcoholic,* the author explains as follows:

> So often people have the misconceived idea that once they have accepted Christ as their Saviour, everything depends upon Him.
>
> Such an attitude is seen in the alcoholic who goes down to the corner bar, praying, "Lord, deliver me from temptation." He orders a drink and sits there, figuratively expecting God to send His angels to remove the drink, somehow pick him up and set him out on the front sidewalk, thus delivering him from temptation. He sits with the drink in his hand for a couple of minutes, and when he doesn't hear the flutter of angels' wings, he pours the drink down. Then he complains, "God didn't deliver me."
>
> This attitude is so often seen in the lives of alcoholics: that the individual does not have to assume responsibility.[1]

We must consent to having the Spirit transform us. To live a new life, we must let Him crucify the old life. "I am crucified with Christ: nevertheless I live; yet not I, but Christ liveth in me" (Galatians 2:20). When Jesus was crucified, He gave up everything of time

---

[1] Jerry G. Dunn, *God Is for the Alcoholic* (Chicago: Moody Press, 1965), p. 149. Quoted by permission.

and sense. But by so doing, He totally defeated Satan. When we have been crucified with Christ—or to use another figure, have "laid all on the altar"—our old life dies, our new life begins, and we are ready to commence the war on sin.

We must let the Spirit remind us that He is present. It is said that people born blind are not altogether happy if sight is suddenly granted them. They realize for the first time how visible they have always been to other people, perhaps not in a favorable light. Sometime our eyes too will be opened, and we will suddenly see how visible we were to the Lord all the time. Let us open our eyes to this fact now. Someone put it this way: "Do you know the Lord so well that you are embarrassed when you sin?"

In the book *Tip Lewis and His Lamp,* Tip was urged by his minister to apologize for something he had said. When Tip asked if the minister knew how hard it would be for him to apologize, the minister replied, "I wonder if you can think how hard it was for your Saviour to listen to your words this noon."

We must make it our business not to sin. When the Holy Spirit frees us from sin, are we then not able to sin? No—we are able not to sin. But the Spirit will not help us if we still waver and cast longing looks in the wrong direction. He will not honor our prayers if we say, "Lead us not into temptation" and then walk right into it. Whatever we do, let us not encourage the devil to tempt us.

We must be patient with ourselves. Falls are not necessary, but sometimes they are a fact. What should we do about them? Learn from them, but also put them behind as quickly as possible. Yes, we have fallen, but the Lord has not. Why should we lie pitying ourselves and dishonoring the Lord when He stands ready to help us get up and go on our way again?

We must practice. It is easy to tell a novice on a bicycle, "Just move ahead, and natural forces will hold you up." But that overlooks the simple fact that he has never done it before. It will take time and work for him to get the feel of the skill. Gyroscopic force can be a mighty thing; in fact, some gyroscopes are used to stabilize ships. But for a child on a bicycle, that force is very gentle, and at first he will hardly know how to detect it and work along with it. Just so, we have to practice in our cooperation with the Spirit.

We must want all that the Spirit has for us, not just some of it. Too often, people want specific remedies from the Lord in neat little packages. They are like a man with completely rundown health who asks the doctor for medicine to cure his stomach problems. A wise doctor will urge the man to get more sleep, eat fresh vegetables, drink plenty of water, and get regular exercise. Improving his overall health will solve many more problems than just the few most troublesome ones. It is all right to ask the Lord for more patience, but do not be surprised if He answers by working on your whole outlook.

Remember, not only must God have all of us; we must have all of Him. He not only *has* the answer to temptation; He *is* the answer. The Physician Himself is the remedy. "Abide in me, and I in you," said Jesus (John 15:4). Without that relationship, we cannot succeed. With it, we need not fail.

> I've tried in vain a thousand ways
> My fears to quell, my hopes to raise;
> But what I need, the Bible says,
> Is ever, only Jesus.
> —James Procter

Chapter Ten

How the Holy Spirit Guides

"And thine ears shall hear a word behind thee, saying, This is the way, walk ye in it" (Isaiah 30:21).

Most people see no reason to be guided by the Holy Spirit. They are not interested in going where He would take them. If you ask them where they are headed, they might reply lightly, "To McDonald's after work" or "To Hawaii next summer." Others might answer in terms of a career: "I want to get a degree in civil engineering and spend my best years working in that field. And, of course, I want to have a comfortable retirement and leave something for my children."

After a bit of reflection on that question, no doubt you would say, "Ultimately I want to go to heaven and be with God in glory forever." Wonderful, and with such an aspiration, no doubt you want God's Spirit to guide you to heaven.

By what route does the Spirit guide?

"The shortest distance between two points," the saying goes, "is a straight line." But there is another saying too: "The longest way around is the shortest way home." With the Spirit guiding you, that is often the truth. Not many people go straight from conversion to glory. The Lord wants to show us some interesting sights along the way. He has some joys for us, some sorrows, some challenges.

This does not mean we should take detours of our own, doing

things the Lord does not want us to do. By the same token, neither should we be taking shortcuts. We must accept the experiences the Lord has chosen for us.

"On our first date," said a man to his wife, "I knew you were the one for me." She asked, "Then why didn't you marry me sooner?" He had his reasons. One was that she was younger than he and needed time to mature. The Lord has His reasons too for withholding certain things from us now, and one of those reasons is that we need time to grow up.

Does the Spirit speak with an audible voice?

It is rare but not unheard of. This writer is personally acquainted with an honest man who once heard an audible voice giving him information he needed to know about his future life. In Acts 8:29, Philip had a similar experience when he came upon an Ethiopian eunuch riding in a chariot. "Then the Spirit said unto Philip, Go near, and join thyself to this chariot." The Spirit's message to Philip's heart was as clear as if it had been audible, and maybe it was audible.

However, we should not expect this kind of experience. The Spirit knows how loudly to speak; and if He is audible, we must take heed. If not, we must still take heed.

Does the Spirit guide by unusual and mysterious means?

Once again, not necessarily. Everyone is led by some spirit. For instance, how does your own spirit guide you? Does it not set goals, draw guidelines, mark out some things to be pursued and some to be avoided, and keep you going when the going gets tough? "The spirit of a man will sustain his infirmity" (Proverbs 18:14). Is there anything mysterious about that?

There is not much mysterious about Satan either. The Bible calls him "the spirit that now worketh in the children of disobedience" (Ephesians 2:2), and anyone can see how he works. Perhaps we can use his methods to cast light on how the Holy Spirit works.

We know by experience that Satan brings evil suggestions to people's minds. The Spirit brings thoughts to people's minds too, but of a holy quality.

We know how Satan uses music and how people follow the suggestions they hear. But the Spirit of the Lord also has music for His people. His music guides our spirits to God in worship and devotion and love. "Be filled with the Spirit; speaking to yourselves in psalms and hymns and spiritual songs, singing and making melody in your heart to the Lord" (Ephesians 5:18, 19).

We know how Satan works through groups. Under his influence, people can stir each other to do things they never would have done alone. "A horrible contagion," someone called it. The Holy Spirit works in groups too. "Where two or three are gathered together in my name," Jesus said, "there am I in the midst of them" (Matthew 18:20). And the Bible reminds us, "Let us consider one another to provoke unto love and to good works" (Hebrews 10:24).

We know how Satan keeps leading people on over a period of time. Who is more defiled than an evil-minded old man? But the Spirit also leads people on. Who is more saintly than someone who has been serving the Lord for many years?

In all these cases, of course, Satan and the Spirit of Christ are working in opposite directions. These examples are given simply to show that the workings of spirits might not be so mysterious as we think.

What are some reliable means of Holy Spirit guidance?

You may have heard the story of a passenger on a ship who asked the pilot how he could guide his ship into the harbor at night. He replied, "Do you see those three lights on the shore? I maneuver the ship until all three lights line up and become as one light. Then I steer the ship straight in."

The Holy Spirit gives us four lights to guide us on our way.

They are the Word of God, the counsel and example of godly people, circumstances, and an inner sense of direction.

The Word of God. This is God's written message to us. We know it comes from God's Spirit because "holy men of God spake as they were moved by the Holy Ghost" (2 Peter 1:21). "All scripture is given by inspiration of God" (2 Timothy 3:16).

Some people try to follow the Bible alone without reference to other believers. It is true that the Bible can stand alone, but it is also true that we are human and can interpret it wrongly. That is why our interpretations must be confirmed by other Christians.

Beware of the attitude, "I just take the Bible for what it says." Anyone can find a favorite text and say, "See, right here it is." School students say that. "I got my answer straight out of the book!" Yes, they got the answer out of the book, but does it answer the question?

The apostle Peter admitted frankly that some writings of Scripture are "hard to be understood, which they that are unlearned and unstable wrest [twist] . . . unto their own destruction" (2 Peter 3:16). Even a Bible scholar can wrest the Scriptures. One young man remarked of some people he knew, "They go back to the Greek and make it say anything they want."

Despite the fact that the Scriptures can be twisted, we still follow the Scriptures. We do not accept the idea of the Catholic Church during the Middle Ages, that the Bible is better kept out of the hands of the common people. Jesus urged, "Search the scriptures; . . . they are they which testify of me" (John 5:39).

In *The Pilgrim's Progress,* Christian and Hopeful came to a fork in the road, followed a stranger's advice, and soon found themselves off the right road and caught in a net. A rescuer set them on the right road and asked them if they had not been given a note by certain shepherds beforehand, telling them which way to go. They admitted that they had. Why then had they not read it? Their sheepish answer was, "We forgot." Yes, the unlearned and unstable do wrest the Scriptures, but the majority of the unlearned and unstable probably forget to study the Scriptures in the first place.

The counsel and example of godly people. Of course, we must sort out the signals we get from others, even kindly and well-meaning people. "Everyone does it" is not good enough because the Bible says, "Thou shalt not follow a multitude to do evil" (Exodus 23:2). Too many people know how to use the power of a group to white-wash an evil. If the Bible condemns what they want to do, they say, "We'll appoint a panel to consider the matter and decide what the Bible really means." You can predict the outcome of that.

But the group can help us considerably. Jesus' disciples did learn from each other. "Can there any good thing come out of Nazareth?" Nathanael asked Philip, and Philip replied, "Come and see" (John 1:46). The conscience of a group, if the group is godly, is always safer than the conscience of one individual. "More than half of the people," it is said, "are right more than half of the time." A church member who ignores this principle does so to his own peril.

Circumstances. Here again, we cannot use this signal alone. Challenge a professing Christian about sin in his life, and he may reply, "But God answers my prayers and blesses my life." Sorry, favorable circumstances are not enough to stake one's spiritual life upon.

The apostle Peter wrote about an experience that was precious to him. He had heard a voice from heaven saying, "This is my beloved Son, in whom I am well pleased." Peter testified, "And this voice which came from heaven we heard, when we were with him in the holy mount." But even an experience like that was not the last word for Peter. He wrote, "We have also a more sure word of prophecy; whereunto ye do well that ye take heed" (2 Peter 1:17–19). That "more sure word" is obviously the Scriptures.

However, circumstances can be very helpful. Jesus used them to point out His will. "Go ye into the city," He said to two disciples, "and there shall meet you a man bearing a pitcher of water: follow him" (Mark 14:13). That was the way they found a house in which to eat the Passover.

David Livingstone once planned to be a missionary to China. God closed doors, and David ended up in Africa. When God closes one door, He opens another; so it is seldom a good idea to run headlong over conflicting circumstances to pursue a pet plan. Certainly we must surmount the inevitable obstacles, but we should be able to sense when God is withholding His blessing.

An inner sense of direction. It might come in a flash, but more likely it will come over a period of time. As a Christian faces decisions, he prays, counsels with others, observes, and thinks; and slowly it becomes clear what he must do. Something tells him, "This is the way, walk ye in it" (Isaiah 30:21). The same instinct protects him from evil. When he hears of something wrong, he might say, "I'm not sure exactly what's wrong with that, but I don't feel good about it."

Of all the Spirit's lights, perhaps the inner sense of direction is the one most easily misunderstood. A sense of direction alone can be completely wrong. Ask any airplane pilot (if he survived) how it worked to fly through a thick cloud by his "inner compass" rather than his instrument panel.

"If you send out ten men to follow the Spirit," one church leader observed dryly, "they'll go ten different directions." The trouble with these ten hypothetical men might be that they think of the Spirit only as an "inner light" and forget that He also works through other Christians, through circumstances, and through His own Word. The same Spirit who gives us a sense of direction has also given these other "charts and instruments." We insult Him if we neglect to use them.

Why do godly people who have the same Spirit sometimes disagree?

By the same token, why do well-behaved children who have good teachers sometimes disagree with each other? It is because they are still children, still learning. They have not "arrived" yet.

Brethren need to discuss things among themselves; that is good for them. When two ministers deal with the same person or group, one might hold out for strong discipline and the other for patience and gentleness. Let each heed the other's concern so that they reach a proper balance. In this way, even though they promote somewhat different spiritual views, they can still "be of the same mind in the Lord" (Philippians 4:2) and help everyone involved.

It is perfectly right for a person to stand up for what he believes. Only let no one claim that he has the last and final revelation on all controversies. "I have the gift of discernment," one man declared, "and I know." Let us be more humble than that, always looking for the Spirit's four lights and knowing that the Spirit Himself will have the final word.

> Brightly doth His Spirit shine
> Into this poor heart of mine;
> While He leads, I cannot fall;
> Trusting Jesus, that is all.
> —*Edgar Page Stites*

Chapter Eleven

When the Holy Spirit Seems to Be Silent

"Why standest thou afar off, O Lord?" (Psalm 10:1).

It is never pleasant to get a rebuff, especially from the Lord. But the Bible tells us of a woman who pleaded for Jesus to help her daughter, and "he answered her not a word" (Matthew 15:23). When a nobleman sought healing for his son, Jesus responded by saying, "Except ye see signs and wonders, ye will not believe" (John 4:48). Jesus' own mother came for help, and He replied, "Woman, what have I to do with thee? mine hour is not yet come" (John 2:4).

Sometimes we feel the way those people must have felt, when we seek the Lord for direction. We look for the lights mentioned in the previous chapter: the Word of God, the counsel and example of godly people, circumstances, and an inner sense of direction. Yet they give no clear answer and sometimes even contradict each other. Why is the Spirit silent?

Maybe He is not silent. It may be that we have not been listening for the right thing. Did you expect some clear manifestation of God's will like a wind, a fire, or an earthquake? Perhaps you failed to listen for a still, small voice (1 Kings 19:11, 12).

God reserves the right to speak with a voice like thunder. But when He speaks to friends, He speaks as true friends speak. They make suggestions, but they would rather nudge than push their point. The Spirit's inner sense of direction can easily be drowned out by the pressure of the moment.

Sometimes His voice does get drowned out. How many times, after making a big mistake, have you said, "I thought something didn't seem quite right!" In light of this, listen before you leap. Turn down the noise, whether outer or inner. Then simply tell the Lord that you are about to make a decision. Present your plan and tell Him that if He has a better one, He is welcome to guide you in that direction. To pray, "Lord, is this what You want?" will not take long. Then do not strain your ears for a "voice," but simply proceed with your plans, remembering that you have asked the Lord to stop you or steer you if He so chooses.

Maybe the Spirit is indeed silent. Sometimes the Lord withdraws somewhat from His children to show His disapproval and make them eager to get back into full fellowship with Him. King Saul felt the sting of this when his relationship with the Lord was slipping. "[God] answered him not that day" (1 Samuel 14:37). Saul realized something was wrong and resorted to casting lots to find direction. He should have been more sincere about getting right with God. His relationship with the Lord continued to deteriorate until he said at the close of life, "God is departed from me, and answereth me no more, neither by prophets, nor by dreams" (1 Samuel 28:15).

The Lord may be wanting us to learn from the first rebuff so we do not lose out completely in our relationship with Him.

Maybe the Spirit is silent because you are too impatient. Do you want the answer before you fully understand the question? That sometimes happens with children in school. They ask the teacher mischievous questions, hoping for a broad enough hint to help them get the answer without much work. A good teacher explains the question first. He tries to get the students to figure things out for themselves. He knows that without the struggle, children will not develop the mental ability they must have by the time they leave school.

Jesus told parables and left the applications for people to figure out. If the disciples failed to understand, He explained the application, but only after they had puzzled over it for a while. Today His Spirit gives us parables in the form of real-life perplexities. We want answers, and He stands back and says in effect, "Puzzle over it awhile!" He knows that without this exercise we will always remain children, simply doing what we are told and perhaps never seeing the underlying principles.

Maybe the Spirit is silent because you are not willing to accept what He has already spoken through His Word. A woman once spoke up in a meeting and told the presiding minister, "The Spirit told me I don't have to wear a head covering." At this, another woman spoke up and said, "The Spirit told me I'm supposed to wear one." The minister replied, "The Spirit didn't tell either one of you; the Bible already gives direction on that subject."[1]

No doubt the minister oversimplified, for the Spirit does illuminate the Bible—even its clear-cut teachings. But the minister had a point. When the Bible has already spoken, the Spirit has already spoken.

Consider another example. In the 1500s, the Anabaptists recognized that believer's baptism is right and infant baptism is wrong. They began to act on their understanding and were baptized as adults. But some people feared persecution and reasoned obedience away. They argued that since the New Testament practice of believer's baptism had been dropped for so long, they ought to wait for some obvious leading from the Lord before observing it again.

The Anabaptists rejected this idea. Pilgram Marpeck wrote, "We

---

[1] 1 Corinthians 11:3–16.

would ask . . . where, when, and for what reason Christ has repealed or abrogated His commands and institutions, or how it came about that His commands could have been nullified to such extent that their observance in the present time must be authorized again by a special command and a divinely manifested special call. Or where and with what words has Christ commanded, if men for a time through disobedience, apostasy, or seduction, neglect and abolish His commands, . . . [that they] should no longer observe them without a special, manifest or miraculous authorization?"[2]

Perhaps the problem is that we do not know what the Bible says. Jesus said that the Spirit would "bring all things to your remembrance, whatsoever I have said unto you" (John 14:26). But the Spirit will not bring to our remembrance things we never learned. We must make it our responsibility to know what the Bible says.

Maybe the Spirit prefers not to show you obvious things. Genesis 21:14–19 tells how Hagar, Sarah's handmaid, went into the wilderness and ran out of water. Her son became faint, and she expected him to die. She left him under a shrub, walked away, and wept. At that point "God opened her eyes, and she saw a well of water." Maybe God had deliberately kept her from seeing the well before, but the angel's question suggests otherwise. "What aileth thee, Hagar?" Perhaps God expected her, by faith in Him, to see more than she had seen.

Sometimes we simply need to see the sensible thing to do, and do it. If your children need shoes, do you wait to go to the shoe store until God tells you to? Of course not. Certainly it would be right to pray about it and pay attention to the circumstances. Maybe there are shoes in the attic that you put there three years ago and forgot about. But just as certainly, the Bible instructs us to provide

---

[2] John Horsch, *Mennonites in Europe* (Crockett, Ky.: Rod and Staff Publishers, Inc., 1995), pp. 136, 137.

for our children's needs. We do not need a special revelation to confirm that.

Maybe the Spirit is silent because He is happy with whatever you decide. After God made Adam, He brought the animals to him "to see what he would call them: and whatsoever Adam called every living creature, that was the name thereof" (Genesis 2:19). Imagine Adam saying, "Lord, what shall I call this one?" The Lord would probably have said, "That is your decision, Adam. If you're satisfied, I am too."

What shall you name the baby? No doubt there are some unsuitable answers, as anyone knows who thumbs through one of those name books! No doubt it is right to pray about the subject. But finally, the decision is yours, and whatsoever you call the child, that shall be the name thereof. If your choice is reasonable, the Lord will be satisfied.

Whom shall you marry? Again, there are unsuitable possibilities. Again, this calls for prayer. But to assume that the Lord has marked out one person whom you must find is not right. Neither is it fair, as a rule, to ask Him for a sign that will tell you which person. One story tells of a young lady who thought the traffic lights in town would be a good way for the Lord to show her if the man she was dating was for her. If the two lights were green when she reached them, she would know the answer was yes. If the lights were red, she would know the answer was no. You guessed it: one light was green and one was red.

"She is at liberty to be married to whom she will," wrote the apostle Paul in 1 Corinthians 7:39, "only in the Lord."

Shall you fast tomorrow? This question does not trouble some people, who simply make up their minds. Others tend to agonize. Here again, there is usually little point in asking the Lord for guidance except in a general way. He will not give you specific instructions. You might think of exactly as many arguments for it as against it. Why? Because the Lord is satisfied either way.

74

We should fast sometimes, health and circumstances permitting. But as a rule, the Spirit will not tell you whether you should fast on Friday, June 16. Unless He gives clear direction one way or another, we need not worry about grieving Him as long as our goal is to please Him.

Likewise, whether we prefer taco salad or mashed potatoes and gravy is not extremely important to God. "He that eateth, eateth to the Lord, for he giveth God thanks; and he that eateth not, to the Lord he eateth not, and giveth God thanks" (Romans 14:6). One saint can decide differently from another as long as his heart is right before God and he does what he does for God's glory.

Should you apologize for something you have said or done? Usually the Lord's will is fairly obvious on such matters. If we have a pretty good idea that we need not mention it, then let us not. If we have a pretty good idea we should make it right, let us do it freely and frankly so we can forget it. In general, getting something off our mind is not nearly as painful as we thought it would be.

But sometimes a question is highly vexatious! The Bible does not seem to speak specifically about the situation, neither do circumstances or the examples of others. Every time you flip a mental coin, it lands on edge. You wonder if you are really being honest with yourself.

Often the thing that troubles people most about such questions is that they fear for their spiritual welfare if they make a mistake. But as we have seen, there are cases when we must simply decide for ourselves. Sometimes we must make arbitrary decisions and move ahead, trusting the Lord to bless as He chooses. We can find rest by saying, "This is what I will do, and I believe the Lord is satisfied. If not, He will make that clear to me."

Other saints too have gone through their times of uncertainty in determining the Lord's will. King David wanted to build a house for the Lord, and he told Nathan the prophet about his plan. Nathan replied, "Go, do all that is in thine heart; for the LORD is with thee" (2 Samuel 7:3). But later the prophet had to change his message because God said that David's son, not David, was to build the temple. God could have given Nathan that message beforehand, but He chose not to. This illustrates the fact that sometimes people must find their way slowly as God leads them along.

In another case, Paul and Silas, traveling through what is now Turkey, "were forbidden of the Holy Ghost to preach the word in Asia" (a Roman province). Later "they assayed to go into Bithynia: but the Spirit suffered them not" (Acts 16:6, 7). Once again, we find ourselves in good company. Paul and Silas might have wanted to pray, "Don't tell us what we shouldn't do; just tell us what we should do!" Eventually the Lord did tell them what to do when He sent the "Macedonian call." But He let His children be mystified for a while beforehand.

There could be any number of reasons why the Spirit remains silent. It might not be our fault at all. He will help us through each day until the answer comes. While waiting for it, we should not force the issue but rest in Him.

Though the Lord is sometimes silent, we can be confident of one thing. He is not giving us the silent treatment, as carnal people sometimes do to one another. Whatever He does, He does for a loving reason; and if we are patient with His processes, sooner or later we will understand. In the meantime, we can sing with new feeling, "Teach me the patience of unanswered prayer."[3]

> Blind unbelief is sure to err
> And scan His work in vain;
> God is His own interpreter,
> And He will make it plain.
> —*William Cowper*

---

[3] George Crowly, "Spirit of God, Descend Upon My Heart."

Chapter Twelve

The Baptism of the Holy Spirit

"For John truly baptized with water; but ye shall be baptized with the Holy Ghost not many days hence" (Acts 1:5).

The New Testament contains at least seven references to the baptism of the Holy Spirit. How is this experience manifested? What are its effects in a believer's life? These questions are addressed in this chapter.

The baptism of the Holy Spirit will vary from one person to another. No one should stipulate beforehand how it will happen for him. And no one, no matter how wonderful his experience, should insist that it must happen the same way for everyone else.

Jesus told Nicodemus, "The wind bloweth where it listeth, and thou hearest the sound thereof, but canst not tell whence it cometh, and whither it goeth: so is every one that is born of the Spirit" (John 3:8). The wind goes where it pleases; we cannot control it. We speak of harnessing the wind, but all we do is place windmills where the wind has already pleased to blow, and the wind obligingly pushes. Neither can we altogether explain the wind. We know in a general way where a wind came from, but no one can set up a signpost and say, "It began here." Even "the sound thereof" will vary from a murmur to a roar.

John the Baptist learned this lesson. He had been told that he would see the Spirit descending on the Son of God. John probably had a mental picture of what he would see; but when the moment came, he was astonished because Jesus came to him to be baptized with water. "I have need to be baptized of thee," said John, "and comest thou to me?" (Matthew 3:14). Jesus, however, assured John that this act would "fulfil all righteousness," so John baptized him. It was then that John saw the sign he was looking for, the Spirit descending like a dove from heaven.

After His resurrection, Jesus promised His disciples, "Ye shall be baptized with the Holy Ghost not many days hence" (Acts 1:5). If they expected a dove to descend again, they were mistaken. This time the Spirit came with the sound of a rushing mighty wind and with tongues like fire and gave them the ability to speak in foreign languages.

That same day, about three thousand more people experienced the baptism of the Holy Spirit. It is hard to know what they were expecting. All they knew was what Peter promised them—that if they would repent and be baptized in the Name of Christ, they would "receive the gift of the Holy Ghost" (Acts 2:38).

What did they receive? Did they also hear wind, see tongues of fire, and speak in tongues? The Bible does not say. But most of us instinctively would reply, "Not necessarily." Their heart experience was similar to that of the apostles, but it probably had a different manifestation. If they saw no fire, they at least had a kindling of spirit—call it a change of attitude, if you please—that could have come only from the Spirit of God. If they could not speak for the Lord in foreign tongues, they at least had a new power to speak for the Lord in their own. Something unexplainable but real had happened. They had come under the power of God and were living under that power.

Next in line for Spirit baptism were the Samaritans, the half-Jews that "real" children of Abraham had looked down on for centuries. Jesus had told His disciples, "Ye shall be witnesses unto me both in Jerusalem, and in all Judaea, and in Samaria" (Acts 1:8).

But to actually go to Samaria and ask God to baptize Samaritans with the Holy Ghost must have been a strange sensation. Nevertheless, Peter and John did just that (Acts 8:14, 15). Perhaps John smiled to himself, remembering that in Samaria he had once asked, "Lord, wilt thou that we command fire to come down from heaven, and consume them, even as Elias did?" (Luke 9:54). He was calling down a different and much better kind of fire now.

After this came an even harder step—one that reminds us of the tensions between blacks and whites in our day. The early Christians were Jews, enjoying the pure, unspoiled presence of the Holy Spirit. Would the Spirit stoop so far as to come upon the *Gentiles*? Jesus had seemed to say so. "Ye shall be witnesses unto me . . . unto the uttermost part of the earth" (Acts 1:8).

When Peter under the Spirit's guidance ventured to preach to Cornelius and his company, "the Holy Ghost fell on all them which heard the word" (Acts 10:44). Peter's companions were astonished "because that on the Gentiles also was poured out the gift of the Holy Ghost. For they heard them speak with tongues, and magnify God" (verses 45, 46). How distant the Gentiles had always seemed from the truth! Yet here they were, speaking with tongues, just as the apostles had done at Pentecost. The Spirit was breaking down their preconceived ideas about the Gentiles.

In Acts 19, some other people also received the Holy Spirit after receiving a new understanding—namely, that there is a Holy Spirit! "We have not so much as heard whether there be any Holy Ghost" they had said (verse 2). But they were open to this new truth, and soon they were enjoying the presence of the Spirit.

Should everyone expect the same manifestation of Spirit baptism that they experienced? Of course not. Many people have experienced moments in their lives when God seemed especially near to them. Their joy and peace were so wonderful that some of them have contended that everyone should have a similar experience. But the Spirit might choose to bless us in another way suited to our own needs; and if that way is not dramatic, we should not think the Spirit has passed us by.

Some people point to the question Paul asked these believers at Ephesus: "Have ye received the Holy Ghost since ye believed?" (Acts 19:2). They imply that each of us should have a similar experience sometime after we first believed. Well, let us pursue that line of thought. Suppose we begin with the words of those believers: "We have not so much as heard whether there be any Holy Ghost." Can you say that? The incident is not quite applicable after all, is it?

Let us go a little further and answer the question, "Unto what then were ye baptized?" Are you ready to answer, "Unto John's baptism"? That does not apply either, because you know more of the Gospel than what John the Baptist taught. In light of this, it seems reasonable to recognize what God did for the believers in Acts 19 without thinking we must have the same for ourselves.

However, we must acknowledge this: many Christians are so woefully ignorant of what God can do in their lives that they are really not much better off than the men who had never heard of the Holy Ghost. Let them pray for what they are missing! Let God do His mighty work in whatever way He chooses.

After receiving the Spirit's baptism, we must not assume that we have nothing more to seek. Our relationship with the Lord cannot be salted, canned, or pickled. It is alive and must grow.

The people on whom the Spirit came had a holy restlessness. Shortly after Jesus had received the dovelike manifestation, "the Spirit driveth him into the wilderness" (Mark 1:12). Jesus was a driven man all through His ministry—not that He objected to this. In fact, He nurtured the flame that drove Him. The Spirit drove Him to cleanse the temple, "and his disciples remembered that it was written, The zeal of thine house hath eaten me up" (John 2:17). The Spirit led Jesus all the way to the cross.

What of the disciples? Always they wanted more. The apostle

Paul cried out, "That I may know him, and the power of his resurrection, and the fellowship of his sufferings, being made conformable unto his death; if by any means I might attain unto the resurrection of the dead. Not as though I had already attained, either were already perfect: but I follow after, if that I may apprehend that for which also I am apprehended of Christ Jesus" (Philippians 3:10–12).

Jesus had said, "Whosoever drinketh of the water that I shall give him shall never thirst; but the water that I shall give him shall be in him a well of water springing up into everlasting life" (John 4:14). Now if the living water is so satisfying, why did Paul want more? It does satisfy; that is why he wanted more! Paul did not turn away and look for something else, as people do when they go from water skiing to mountain climbing to photography to antiques. He went back for more of the same because it satisfied.

This does not mean that we seek repeated baptisms of the Spirit. When a person is converted, he is just as born again as he will ever be. In that sense, he has as much of the Spirit as he will ever have. But his acquaintance with the Spirit, his love for the Lord, his sensitivity to the Lord's will—these grow and should continue to grow on into eternity.

Not only are we unable to specify how the Spirit will come, but we also cannot define how the Spirit will continue to work in our lives after He has arrived. Quite often what people need is not to get more of the Spirit, as they always thought, but to let the Spirit get more of them. The experiences that bring this about are anything but glorious. Instead of speaking in tongues, they get their foot in their mouth. Instead of hearing the sound of a rushing mighty wind, they feel the frustration of inadequacy. Instead of glowing tongues of fire, they feel the heat of shame over mistakes they have made. A crumbling process takes place, which is just what the Spirit wants. The more the child of God crumbles, the more freedom the Spirit has to work.

It is interesting what Paul had to say about this subject after he

81

had pleaded with the Lord to remove the thorn in his flesh. "And he said unto me, My grace is sufficient for thee: for my strength is made perfect in weakness. Most gladly therefore will I rather glory in my infirmities, that the power of Christ may rest upon me" (2 Corinthians 12:9). Again he said, "But we have this treasure in earthen vessels, that the excellency of the power may be of God, and not of us" (2 Corinthians 4:7).

Observe the word *power* in both passages. Sometimes while we are gazing in one direction, looking for power, the Spirit slips it into our lives from another. While we are praying for a blessing such as someone else has had, we get a thorn in the flesh (or something else; it is not always painful) that turns out to be the answer to our prayer for blessing. While we wish for power to get the Spirit to do what we want Him to do, He purges that thought from us and gives us power to do what *He* wants *us* to do.

It bears repeating that none of us—not one, no matter how spiritual—ever comes to the point where there is nothing more to seek. A man who joined a church new to him remarked that in his new church he was called a "seeker." He wondered if the people already there thought they were "havers." They should have been havers; we should all be. But we must be seekers too.

Remember what Paul said. "I follow after [press on], if that I may apprehend that for which also I am apprehended of Christ Jesus" (Philippians 3:12). To apprehend is to arrest or get hold of. When Christ arrested us, He had something in mind for us to seize in turn. Paul was saying, "I want to get hold of all the Lord had in mind for me when He got hold of me!"

That should be our ambition as well, along with what Paul said next. "Brethren, I count not myself to have apprehended: but this one thing I do, forgetting those things which are behind, and reaching forth unto those things which are before, I press toward the mark for the prize of the high calling of God in Christ Jesus" (Philippians 3:13, 14).

I'm pressing on the upward way,
New heights I'm gaining ev'ry day;
Still praying as I'm onward bound,
"Lord, plant my feet on higher ground."
                    —*Johnson Oatman, Jr.*

Chapter Thirteen

How Do We Know
We Have the Holy Spirit?

"Now if any man have not the Spirit of Christ, he is none of his" (Romans 8:9).

Jesus was a very positive person. Although He could see shades of gray, He had little time for people who wanted to see gray when the issues were black and white. He went around assuring people either that they were on the right track or that they were not.

To the Pharisees, He said, "Ye serpents, ye generation of vipers, how can ye escape the damnation of hell?" (Matthew 23:33). But to a seeking lawyer, He said, "Thou art not far from the kingdom of God" (Mark 12:34). After Peter confessed that Jesus is the Christ, He said, "Blessed art thou, Simon Barjona: for flesh and blood hath not revealed it unto thee, but my Father which is in heaven" (Matthew 16:17).

To Zacchaeus, who declared he would make his wrongs right and live a new life, Jesus said, "This day is salvation come to this house" (Luke 19:9). To a dying thief who said, "Lord, remember me when thou comest into thy kingdom," Jesus said, "Verily I say unto thee, To day shalt thou be with me in paradise" (Luke 23:42, 43). Not surprisingly, the Spirit of Christ still assures people either that they are righteous or that they are sinful.

Why assurance is needed. Why is it important to the Lord that godly people be assured of their salvation? And why is assurance important to us? Maybe that is too obvious a question, since everyone wants assurance and security. But we will consider several reasons why we need to be assured of our right relationship with God.

Assurance gives us a reason to struggle against temptation. If we are under God's smile as we struggle, we feel like striving on. If we are under God's frown no matter what we do, what is the point of trying? That is one good reason to study this subject. Far too many discouraged people decide that God does not care about their struggles against sin, so they give up.

Assurance gives us confidence in testifying. We cannot expect to persuade sensible people by saying, "Come along with me to where I think I'm going." A calm and confident testimony is much more convincing.

Assurance is pleasant, and God wants our lives to be pleasant along this line. Anyone knows the value of assurance if he has lost his way in a strange city, or has climbed a shaky ladder, or has gathered all his courage to ask a young lady for her friendship. Once he has received directions from a passerby, or has firmly fastened the ladder with a rope, or hears a willing yes from the person who might have said no, he feels much better.

It is also highly pleasant when someone who fears the Judgment Day finds peace with God and begins looking forward to seeing Him face to face. On one hand, "fear hath torment" (1 John 4:18). On the other, "ye have received the Spirit of adoption, whereby we cry, Abba, Father" (Romans 8:15; see also Galatians 4:6, 7). *Abba* is a term of endearment something like "Daddy" or "Papa."

How assurance is gained. When people want assurance of a thing, they go to great lengths to obtain it. "Do you have two forms of ID?" "What is your password?" "Your date of birth?" "And your mother's maiden name?" Corporate and government officers do not judge the truth of our words by general impressions; they must have something solid to go by.

What is the solid evidence that assures us of salvation? Actually, that is the wrong question to ask first. The right one is, What satisfies God? What is it, when He looks upon us, that marks us as His own?

It is simply His own presence in our lives in the person of the Holy Spirit. When God looks at a saint, He sees something of Himself. Once God is assured of our salvation, our own assurance is natural because it is based on fact.

The second question is this: When we look at our own lives, what marks us as His own? The same thing does—the Holy Spirit, God's presence in our lives. "Hereby know we that we dwell in him, and he in us, because he hath given us of his Spirit" (1 John 4:13).

This is considerably more than a card or certificate that we carry around and pull out when we need it. This is a companion. This is the friendship of God Himself. Indeed, it is a foretaste of the glories to come. We know that the presence of God is what makes heaven out of heaven. When God gives a little of Himself to us, He gives a little of heaven.

The Scriptures support the idea that the Holy Spirit is a foretaste of heaven. "After that ye believed, ye were sealed with that holy Spirit of promise, which is the earnest of our inheritance" (Ephesians 1:13, 14). An earnest is a down payment, but *earnest* also expresses the idea well. God has an inheritance for us; and to assure us that He is *in earnest* about eventually giving it to us, He gives us a little of it now. What is the inheritance? It is for us to be with Him eternally in glory. What is the down payment? For Him to be with us in the meantime—"Christ in you, the hope of glory" (Colossians 1:27).

One question remains. When we have a companion to travel with us, we know he is there because we see him. We say we have God's Spirit to be our companion. But how do we know for sure?

For some people, there might be dramatic evidences at first.

Cornelius and his companions spoke in tongues. However, there is no evidence that all New Testament converts spoke in tongues or that the apostles encouraged them to do so. Neither is it likely that Cornelius and his friends spoke in tongues for the rest of their lives. In fact, the only people who made much of speaking in tongues after the initial Spirit baptism were the Corinthians—and Paul went to considerable lengths to correct their misguided ideas on the matter.

What about the other gifts of the Spirit? Many people put great emphasis on things like wisdom, knowledge, faith, gifts of healing, miracles, prophecy, speaking in tongues, and interpretation of tongues (1 Corinthians 12:8–10). These all have been good and right in their place. But Jesus set these things in perspective when He said, "Many will say to me in that day, Lord, Lord, have we not prophesied in thy name? and in thy name have cast out devils? and in thy name done many wonderful works? And then will I profess unto them, I never knew you: depart from me, ye that work iniquity" (Matthew 7:22, 23).

Where the Spirit is present, there are spiritual gifts; but where gifts are, the Spirit may or may not be present.

What evidences of the Spirit should always be present?

Obedience to the Word of the Spirit (the Bible). We noted before that the apostle John wrote, "Hereby know we that we dwell in him, and he in us, because he hath given us of his Spirit" (1 John 4:13). John wrote some other things too. "And hereby we do know that we know him, if we keep his commandments" (1 John 2:3). And again, "If ye know that he is righteous, ye know that every one that doeth righteousness is born of him" (1 John 2:29). "Little children, let no man deceive you: he that doeth righteousness is righteous, even as he is righteous" (1 John 3:7).

A Christlike acceptance of other people. "He that saith he is in the light, and hateth his brother, is in darkness even until now. He

87

that loveth his brother abideth in the light, and there is none occasion of stumbling in him" (1 John 2:9, 10). Easily enough we mentally forgive the dying thief of Luke 23 (he never stole from us) or the woman taken in adultery in John 8 (she never sullied anyone we knew). Loving one's brother in spite of his foolishness or in spite of his being a little too severe with us—that is the problem. But that is also the evidence. If the Spirit's love for that brother or sister flows out of us at such crucial times, it is reason to believe that the Spirit owns and controls us.

Acceptance by spiritual people. Spirit-filled people tend to recognize other Spirit-filled people. If other godly people accept you as one of themselves, you may take that as one evidence that you yourself are spiritual. On the day of Pentecost, each person could see the tongues as of fire on other people much better than he could see them on himself.

The fruit of the Spirit. You can find the fruit of the Spirit described in Galatians 5:22, 23. When Paul listed these virtues, he did not mean that no other virtues could be mentioned. He could have talked about perseverance, hope, a teachable spirit, and more. But these nine are a fair sample. Some days, we might think we are not getting much accomplished for the Lord. Are they fruitless days? Not if we show love, joy, peace, long-suffering, and other traits that Jesus showed when He was here on earth.

Victory over sin. "For if ye live after the flesh, ye shall die: but if ye through the Spirit do mortify the deeds of the body, ye shall live (Romans 8:13). "This I say then, Walk in the Spirit, and ye shall not fulfil the lust of the flesh" (Galatians 5:16). The Spirit does not make it easy to battle against sin, but He does make the battle winnable. He does not guarantee that you will never sin again, but He promises, "Sin shall not have dominion over you" (Romans 6:14).

A desire to share Christ with others. "Ye shall receive power, after that the Holy Ghost is come upon you," Jesus promised. For what purpose? "Ye shall be witnesses unto me" (Acts 1:8). Not all of us will be out knocking on doors, but neither will we be content simply to enjoy the wonder of the Spirit in our hearts without sharing it when we get the chance.

A transformed heart. "For they that are after the flesh do mind the things of the flesh; but they that are after the Spirit the things of the Spirit" (Romans 8:5). What do you talk about? Where does your mind turn when it is free to go where it pleases?

Many so-called Christians have the world in their hearts. Non-Christians look at them and see that their interests have not been transformed. Once in a while, those non-Christians do meet a genuine Christian, but they decide he is no different—just a better hypocrite. They might even say, "He can't possibly enjoy living like that; and when no one is looking, he probably doesn't." They fail to realize that once the Spirit gets into people, He gives them a new nature. But when you realize it and have experienced it, this gives you confidence that you are right with God.

Joy, a part of the Spirit fruit. "And the disciples were filled with joy, and with the Holy Ghost" (Acts 13:52). "For the kingdom of God is not meat and drink; but righteousness, and peace, and joy in the Holy Ghost" (Romans 14:17). The "joy of the Holy Ghost" is also mentioned in 1 Thessalonians 1:6. The Holy Ghost is joyful—a new thought to some of us—and so will we be if we have His presence within us. This joy survives our griefs, injuries, and frustrations; it keeps our spirits from totally sinking in our worst moments, and it adds more luster to the day in our best moments.

The witness of the Spirit. "The Spirit itself beareth witness with our spirit, that we are the children of God" (Romans 8:16). He speaks not only through the evidences listed above but also directly to our hearts. He gives an inner testimony that all is well between us and Himself.

Someone may ask, "How does it feel?" The only answer we can give is, "It doesn't feel." How does your sense of balance feel? Could you describe it to someone? Hardly. Yet you probably remember sometime in childhood when you whirled in circles until the floor tilted under you and you felt safer sitting than standing. You remember how *that* felt. You remember too what it was like when the Spirit's quiet approval changed to disapproval because of something you had done, and you could not rest easy until you made the matter right. You surely know how that felt.

One important fact remains. After weighing all the proofs, we still have to take the Spirit's presence by faith. This is not as mysterious as it may sound. At the bank, we often make transactions without seeing any cash changing hands. The bank gives the evidence on a piece of paper; the figures are there, and that is all. We accept it by faith. When the Lord gives us evidences like those named above, He expects us to trust Him too. Believe that the Spirit is in you—but many people fail right there. The Spirit's work in our hearts is not complete until we can say in faith, "Thank You, God, for the abiding presence of the Holy Ghost."

> How silently, how silently,
>   The wondrous gift is giv'n!
> So God imparts to human hearts,
>   The blessings of His heav'n.
> No ear may hear His coming,
>   But in this world of sin,
> Where meek souls will receive Him still,
>   The dear Christ enters in.
>   —*Phillips Brooks*

Chapter Fourteen

How Do We Keep the Holy Spirit?

"Quench not the Spirit" (1 Thessalonians 5:19).

One of the saddest stories in the Old Testament begins majestically enough. King Saul had the rare and priceless privilege of the Holy Spirit's coming on him and turning him into another man (1 Samuel 10:6). No better crown could have descended on him than that. Under the Spirit's power, Saul showed a unique combination of humility and leadership that catches our imagination and wins our affection for him even today.

Then he committed several serious transgressions, and the time came when "the Spirit of the LORD departed from Saul" (1 Samuel 16:14). His subsequent depressions, spells of near insanity, and final suicide made a deep impression on the next king, David. After he himself had sinned, he pleaded in his psalm of penitence, "Take not thy holy spirit from me" (Psalm 51:11). Perhaps he was remembering not only Saul but also Samson, who lost his superhuman strength and "wist not that the LORD was departed from him" (Judges 16:20).

In the New Testament, we find the same principle. Jesus told of ten virgins who took their lamps and went forth to meet the bridegroom. Five took extra oil with them; five did not. It is often suggested that the oil in this context represents the Holy Spirit. (See Chapter 22 of this book.) When five of the virgins let their oil run out, their relationship with the bridegroom ran out too. The language in this story is restrained, but the symbolism runs deep. It represents the worst disaster that could happen to anyone who has the Holy Spirit—that by not keeping up his relationship with the Lord, he could finally hear the words, "Verily I say unto you, I know you not" (Matthew 25:12).

How can we prevent such a tragedy from happening to us?

Do what made Him welcome in the first place. We answered His knock, and He entered our hearts. Now we continue to answer when He seeks our attention. Remember, He is just as polite now as when He first knocked. He will not force His way. We must willingly hear His voice if we want His continued presence in our lives.

Spend time in the Lord's presence. How do we keep up our acquaintance with friends? By spending time with them, talking to them, letting them talk to us. "Take time to be holy, speak oft with thy Lord; / Abide in Him always, and feed on His Word."[1] Lift your heart to Him from time to time throughout the day. This does not mean we should avoid our daily business, which can actually draw us closer to the Lord. But we should avoid allurements away from His presence. For just one illustration, bypass the gaudy paperback novels, even the used ones you can buy for a nickel. If you read them, you will lose much more in terms of the Lord's companionship than you might gain in terms of reading thrills.

"Walk in the Spirit" (Galatians 5:25). If that sounds mystical, put it this way: walk *in step with* the Spirit, who is none other than the Spirit of Christ. Behave as Jesus behaved when He was here, even as He wants to behave within you now. "He that saith he abideth in him ought himself also so to walk, even as he walked" (1 John 2:6).

---

[1] William D. Longstaff, "Take Time to Be Holy."

Welcome the Spirit's guidance without fear. Do you have any remorse for letting Him lead you in the past? The sins He convicted you of—are you sorry you confessed them and overcame them? What about the times He led you to do things that were very hard—do you regret now that you did them? Then why fear the future?

> Be still, my soul: thy God doth undertake
> To guide the future as He has the past.
> Thy hope, thy confidence let nothing shake;
> All now mysterious shall be bright at last.
> —*Katharina von Schlegel*

When He points out sin, get rid of it. Keep up this process even if it is painful and humiliating and you think you should have outgrown it. Our own discomfort does not matter; what really matters is that we "grieve not the holy Spirit of God, whereby [we] are sealed unto the day of redemption" (Ephesians 4:30).

Do not fear becoming fanatical. Many fanatical things have been done in the Name of the Holy Spirit, but that is not the Spirit's fault. Remember, He is the Spirit of Christ, who was the sanest man that ever lived. Remember too that the Spirit inspired the words, "Let all things be done decently and in order" (1 Corinthians 14:40). Of course, there may be times when you do things that seem fanatical to other people, but that does not mean you are a fanatic. When the house is on fire, it is the sane people who get excited. The insane man sits back and smiles.

Let Him continue to fill you as you grow. The Spirit is alive, just as we are. He does not want to be kept in a small container indefinitely. "Jesus increased in wisdom and stature, and in favour with God and man" (Luke 2:52), and He wants us to do the same.

Let Him keep you. We speak of how to keep the Holy Spirit because we naturally think of our own responsibility first. But the fact is, we do not keep the Holy Spirit. We only welcome Him, and He keeps us. We did not knock on His door; He knocked on ours. We did not seal our own salvation; the Spirit is the one "whereby [we] are sealed unto the day of redemption" (Ephesians 4:30).

Life in the Spirit is much like physical life. To nurture physical life, we do our part by eating, drinking, sleeping, and working. Life then preserves our bodies; no decay sets in as long as life and health remain. The Lord's promise to the church at Philadelphia was, "Because thou hast kept the word of my patience, I also will keep thee" (Revelation 3:10). The same principle holds true for us today.

> From Him who loves me now so well,
> What pow'r my soul can sever?
> Shall life or death, or earth or hell?
> No; I am His forever.
> —James G. Small

Chapter Fifteen

What Happened at Pentecost?

"He hath shed forth this, which ye now see and hear"
(Acts 2:33).

"What happened at Pentecost?" is another way of saying, "What happened to God's power? What changed about the way God's power worked, starting on that day?" There are perhaps a number of answers, but we will consider two.

At Pentecost, the power moved from outside to inside. Jesus made an intriguing statement the night before His crucifixion. "And he said unto them, When I sent you without purse, and scrip, and shoes, lacked ye any thing? And they said, Nothing. Then said he unto them, But now, he that hath a purse, let him take it, and likewise his scrip: and he that hath no sword, let him sell his garment, and buy one. . . . And they said, Lord, behold, here are two swords. And he said unto them, It is enough" (Luke 22:35, 36, 38).

This passage is hard to explain. Why, after saying every man should have a sword, was He content with only two? Why, after Peter tried to use a sword, did Jesus rebuke him and say, "All they that take the sword shall perish with the sword" (Matthew 26:52)?

It appears that Jesus was telling His disciples that things would be different now. They would be thrown upon their own resources. Before then, they could always run to Jesus when in trouble, like the time they nearly perished on the stormy sea (Mark 4:37–39);

or they could hope He would show up, like the time they could not cast out a demon (Mark 9:14–29). Now He would be gone, and they would need to draw from some inner power.

The disciples were never in worse trouble than the night Jesus' enemies took Him away. In fact, even when His physical presence was still with them, they were already failing. They slept when Jesus had said, "Tarry ye here, and watch" (Mark 14:34). Shortly "they all forsook him, and fled" (Mark 14:50) because they had so little inner power. Peter, who probably had greater inner fortitude than the rest, failed the most miserably of them all.

At least their failure may have served a good purpose because it made them realize their need of something they did not have. But to diagnose is not to prescribe. What would solve their problem? The answer arrived some fifty days later, when the Spirit came upon them. Now they no longer needed the physical presence of Jesus to help them along because they had a new power inside.

Other examples illustrate the same principle. Moving from childhood to adulthood, we no longer have to be taken from place to place and be told what to do and how and why. This is as our parents desire it. There comes a time when they are no longer honored by our clinging to them. Rather, they want us to respond to the training they have given us and work it out from the inside.

For another example, God fed the children of Israel manna in the wilderness for forty years. Finally they moved out of the wilderness into the Promised Land, and the manna ceased. They had to plant grain and harvest it, pick grapes, gather olives, and much more. They had to live by their own means. But that was no hardship; the resources were right there, so it was a privilege.

One more illustration: think of the old days when sailing ships traveled the ocean. When the wind blew, they moved. When the wind dropped, they stopped. With the coming of the steamship, things changed. Now ships no longer had to wait for the wind, because an inner power moved them forward.

This is what Pentecost did for the believers in the upper room. They girded on swords; they assumed adulthood; they entered the Promised Land; they received inner power. The "cloven tongues like as of fire" soon disappeared, but it was understood that the real fire was still there.

At Pentecost, the power moved from the few to the many. In Old Testament times, God gave His Spirit to relatively few people for specific purposes. His Spirit would come upon a judge, and he would lead the children of Israel. For example, under the Spirit's direction, Gideon blew a trumpet; and in the following days, thousands of men gathered to help him fight the Midianites. God gave His Spirit to various prophets as well. Elisha requested and received a double portion of Him (2 Kings 2:9, 15).[1]

Some people wished that God's gift of the Spirit were more common and that all could enjoy it. One of these was Moses, who was told by a breathless servant that several men were prophesying out in the camp. "Enviest thou for my sake?" asked Moses. "Would God that all the LORD's people were prophets, and that the LORD would put his spirit upon them!" (Numbers 11:29).

Moses' wish was finally granted when the fire fell at Pentecost. The Spirit came not only upon the people in the upper room; He is a gift for all. The fire fell on the whole church, of whom the handful in the upper room were mere representatives. Peter confirmed this when he said, "Repent, and be baptized every one of you in the name of Jesus Christ for the remission of sins, and ye shall receive the gift of the Holy Ghost. *For the promise is unto you, and to your children, and to all that are afar off, even as many as the Lord our God shall call"* (Acts 2:38, 39).

---

[1] The "spirit of Elijah" came from God in the first place and was given to Elisha, not by Elijah, but by God. It was the Spirit of God.

Joel had prophesied this, and Peter acknowledged it. "But this is that which was spoken by the prophet Joel; And it shall come to pass in the last days, saith God, I will pour out of my Spirit upon all flesh: and your sons and your daughters shall prophesy, and your young men shall see visions, and your old men shall dream dreams: and on my servants and on my handmaidens I will pour out in those days of my Spirit; and they shall prophesy" (Acts 2:16–18). Notice the wide range of people on whom the Spirit would fall: old and young, men and women, even servants and handmaidens. No one need miss this blessing.

Curiously, the things that happened at Pentecost were not altogether identical to the things Joel had predicted. We have no record that anyone had visions or dreams. Neither did the rest of Joel's prophecy come specifically true that day: "And I will shew wonders in heaven above, and signs in the earth beneath; blood, and fire, and vapour of smoke: the sun shall be turned into darkness, and the moon into blood" (Acts 2:19, 20). What was the Holy Ghost signifying by all this?

Not only would the Spirit fall upon a wide range of people, but He would also give them a wide range of gifts. If all the things Joel prophesied had come true at Pentecost, no doubt people would have settled back and said, "This is it. The prophecy is fulfilled." They might have assumed there was nothing more to seek. As it was, people must have realized that they had experienced only a sampling of the things that Joel had described. The events at Pentecost were not the whole story. There was no limit to the things the Spirit might do in the age He had just ushered in.

What does this mean for us? It means that we should see possibilities. We have a tendency either to look right over the small possibilities at our feet, hoping for something "out there," or to wrap our familiar little activities around us and ignore new ways in which we could serve the Lord. Why not dream some dreams? Why not see some visions?

You cannot expect to see Jacob's ladder, but you might see that someone in the group needs a songbook that you can spare or share. That is a small vision. Depending on your place in life, you might see that some distant land needs the Gospel and financial aid, and you might spearhead a movement in answer to the call. That would be a big vision. Most of our visions fall somewhere between these two examples. Let us not hang back when the Lord has a vision for us.

Perhaps other people can learn from your visions. If you have a concern or something you think is a wonderful idea, share it. Introduce it, if you like, by saying, "This might be a foolish idea." If it is foolish, accept that fact and move on. But sometimes the Lord uses even a poorly conceived idea to open the door to a good one. "Your sons and your daughters shall prophesy" (Joel 2:28). This suggests that not only a few gray-haired prophets have something to contribute to the discussion, but that many people do.

Learn from other people's visions too. "Despise not prophesyings" (1 Thessalonians 5:20). One vision leads to another, and so it should. Think of Joel's prophecy like this: "Your old men shall dream dreams, [and so] your young men shall see visions" (Joel 2:28). Old men's dreams often become young men's visions. On the other hand, think of Peter's words like this: "Your young men shall see visions, and [so] your old men shall dream dreams" (Acts 2:17). Young men's visions can rekindle old men's dreams.

Did the coming of the Spirit mean that the signs and wonders which took place at Pentecost would continue all through the church age? Here we must be careful to explain without explaining away. The answer most of us readily give is no. Truly, the disciples did not live the rest of their years with the sound of a rushing mighty wind and the flicker of flame. Neither did they always perform miracles, even when they might have wished to do so (2 Timothy 4:20).

We should not feel alarmed about this. God moves in dramatic ways only at special times for special purposes. Where is the sunrise at noon? It has faded away because the sun has risen. The celebration is over, but the sunshine is here. If we had sunrise all day, it would become commonplace. Where is the wedding twenty years after the wedding day? The moment is over; the marriage continues.

Yet Pentecost keeps on tantalizing people today. They wonder, "Was there something back at Pentecost that God meant for us to keep, which we have lost?" For some churchgoers, the answer is a decided yes. They have lost not only the sunrise but also much of the sun itself. Not only is the wedding over, but the marriage is almost gone. The only answer is to go back—not to Pentecost but to the Lord, who can revive us again. In some instances, He pleases to give His people a revival so spectacular that they are reminded of Pentecost.

Possibly all of us, no matter how close to the Lord, should keep on being tantalized by Pentecost. Perhaps Paul was thinking of Pentecost when he wrote, "This one thing I do, forgetting those things which are behind, and reaching forth unto those things which are before, I press toward the mark for the prize of the high calling of God in Christ Jesus" (Philippians 3:13, 14). It is interesting that he did not propose to turn the clock back to the day of Pentecost. The moment of Pentecost was behind him. But some of the blessing of Pentecost still lay before him. He had learned much from the Lord, but still his prayer was "Deeper, deeper, higher, higher."

This is the meaning of Pentecost—that God uses all sorts of people in all sorts of ways, provided they fit the Bible pattern. Pentecost is for all. Pentecost is for you and me.

> Accept my talents, great or small,
> Choose Thou the path for me,
> Where I shall labor joyously
> In service, Lord, for Thee.
> —*Edith Witmer*[2]

---

[2] *Life Songs, No. 2* (1938; reprint, Ephrata, Pa.: Eastern Mennonite Publications, 1996), #301. Used by permission.

Chapter Sixteen

Learning From Revivals in History

*"Then said they among the heathen, The L*ORD *hath done great things for them" (Psalm 126:2).*

"Ponder the path of thy feet," says Proverbs 4:26. In practical terms, do not embrace everything that sounds good as soon as you hear of it. If the thing is good, it will stand the test of time, and we can then accept it because it is obviously good.

One thing that always sounds good at first is the word *revival*. Right away we think of someone like John Wesley, who preached to crowds of English laborers in the open air and drastically changed England. Or we think of D. L. Moody, the businessman-turned-evangelist whose preaching persuaded thousands to profess faith in Jesus Christ.[1]

Naturally, people who hear of revivals in other times and other places want the same for their own churches. Would it not be wonderful to have such a mighty moving of the Spirit, that neighborhood people would come flocking in to confess their sins and be converted?

But is that the definition of revival—to bring many people in to get saved and on their way to glory? That is one kind of revival,

---

[1]   A number of prominent men are quoted in this chapter, but that does not indicate approval of everything they believed and taught.

and hardly anyone considers it less than a highly desirable kind! However, the testimony of one minister is startling: "In our congregation, we had a great revival, and half the people left." What he wanted and what he got were two different things, but he still claimed revival.

So what definition fits every revival? Charles Finney, one of the most successful revivalists in early American history, put it well. "A revival is nothing else than a new beginning of obedience to God."[2]

Too easily we think of revival merely as expansion of the church as it already is, producing more of the same. But false religions like Islam and Hinduism also have revivals. Does that draw anyone closer to God? No, the believers multiply, but in the end there are only more believers in the wrong religion.

If expansion is all we want, perhaps we should not want revival at all—unless of course the church is so pure that it cannot be improved. Like Paul before Agrippa, we should want others to be as we are. But what does that mean? Not that they should stop where we are at our present level of spiritual attainment, but that they should join us in pressing on to higher ground. All revivals should help us in that direction.

Having established that "a revival is nothing else than a new beginning of obedience to God," how do we get a revival if we need one?

According to an article by R. A. Torrey, a prominent fundamentalist of the past, the most important element in launching a revival is PRAYER (the capitals being his).[3] Torrey's reasons are

---

2   Charles Finney, *Finney on Revival* (Minneapolis: Bethany House Publishers), p. 9.

3   R. A. Torrey, "The Place of Prayer in Evangelism," *Sword and Trumpet,* third quarter, 1951, pp. 5–11.

convincing, as are his illustrations. David Brainerd, missionary to the American Indians in the 1700s, spent many hours in prayer, and his earnest pleas were answered. On one occasion he preached through a drunk interpreter because he could find no one better. Yet to that sermon, scores of Indians responded.

However, even prayer can be useless or deceptive. Jesus warned us not to pray "as the heathen do: for they think that they shall be heard for their much speaking" (Matthew 6:7). Many people who have spent hour after hour in prayer have little to show for it. They might even feel inordinately good about their religious experience because, after all, they prayed. A woman remarked of a man she knew, "He can really pray." But someone else who knew the man replied sadly, "Yes, and live in sin."

Jonathan Goforth, Canadian missionary to China, paid attention not only to prayer but also to something else that we easily forget. When he came to a community for revivals, he would start with the missionaries themselves and try to make sure they were right with the Lord. He wrote, "We cannot emphasize too strongly our conviction that all hindrance in the Church is due to sin. . . . It is sin in individual church members, whether at home or on the foreign field, which grieves and quenches the Holy Spirit."[4]

We are back to our previous definition of revival: "A revival is nothing else than a new beginning of obedience to God." Obedience is what revival is, and obedience is how to get it. Revivals begin with obedience and end with more of the same. If you want to help revive other people's obedience, start by reviving your own.

After that, prayer comes into the picture. "If I regard iniquity in my heart, the Lord will not hear me" (Psalm 66:18). But if I cleanse iniquity from my heart, then I can pray for revival, for God's Word says, "Call unto me, and I will answer thee, and shew thee

---

[4] Jonathan Goforth, *By My Spirit* (Grand Rapids: Zondervan Publishing House, 1942), p. 13.

great and mighty things, which thou knowest not" (Jeremiah 33:3).

One more question comes up. What is this new beginning of obedience to God based upon? Is it not based upon the Bible? Since we are to obey the Bible, must we not then be familiar with it? Once again, church history is full of testimonies from successful Christians that earnest Bible study was one secret of their spiritual prosperity.

But we must avoid the trap of thinking that Bible study alone can save us. Many false cultists study the Bible as much as we do and can quote chapter and verse to support their doctrines. They know the words, but not the Word. Neither do they know the Lord, who gave the Bible. A songwriter put it succinctly: "Beyond the sacred page / I seek *Thee,* Lord."[5] Jesus urged His opponents, "Search the scriptures; for in them ye think ye have eternal life: and they are they which testify of me" (John 5:39). If we study the Bible and keep the Lord in view, we will not go wrong.

Thus we have a three-point outline for revival: (1) repentance and obedience, (2) prayer, and (3) Bible study. Of course the three overlap, and of course much more could be said; but this is the essence of revival.

On this basis, we can learn from every revival we hear about. We can tell whether to take it as an inspiration or only as an example of what not to do.

Perhaps the most outstanding revival in history since Pentecost was the Reformation. Did it include these three points? It certainly did. The printing press brought the Bible to every man, at least to every man who wanted it. The fact that people read and knew what the Bible said was not revival in itself, but it helped break the ground for revival.

Then some daring souls began stepping out and acting on what

---

[5]   Mary Ann Lathbury, "Break Thou the Bread of Life."

they had learned. It was not that they had learned everything they needed to know, but that they obeyed what they did know. Result: the Reformation.

Did prayer enter the picture? Although we do not read whole chapters entitled "Prayers of the Reformation," prayers were certainly interwoven. The Anabaptists, who went further than others in obedience to the Word, certainly prayed. Note the following account:

> And it further came to pass, as they were assembled together, that great anxiety came upon them and they were moved in their hearts. Then they unitedly bowed their knees before God Almighty in heaven and called upon Him, the searcher of all hearts, and implored Him to grant them grace to do His Divine will, and that He would bestow upon them His mercy. . . .

> After they had risen from their prayer George Blaurock arose and earnestly asked Conrad Grebel to baptize him with the true Christian baptism upon his faith and knowledge. . . . And entreating him thus he knelt down, and Conrad baptized him, since there was at that time no ordained minister to administer this ordinance. After this was done, the others likewise asked George to baptize them. He fulfilled their desire in sincere fear of God, and thus they gave themselves unitedly to the name of the Lord. Then some of them were chosen for the ministry of the gospel, and they began to teach and to keep the faith. Thus began the separation from the world and from its evil works.[6]

Although the Reformation began bravely, not all the reformers carried the revival through to fulfillment in complete obedience. But enough impetus had been given that the effects never died out. Even today we enjoy many blessings that began with the few who did carry obedience to its fulfillment. How often we have heard the

---

[6]   Quoted in *Mennonites in Europe,* pp. 50, 51.

quotation, "The lines are fallen unto me in pleasant places; yea, I have a goodly heritage" (Psalm 16:6). God give us the grace to preserve it.

Since Reformation days, a number of Protestant revivals have caught public attention. Besides the men already mentioned, we could include George Whitefield, Jonathan Edwards, Charles Spurgeon, and others. What can we learn from these? Simply this, that to the extent that they led people to "a new beginning of obedience to God," they were successful. To the extent that they passed over this, they were not.

Let us again consider Jonathan Goforth. We stand virtually open-mouthed at the astonishing success of the revivals in China during the early 1900s when Goforth served as evangelist. Stolid men who would never have admitted wrongdoing under ordinary circumstances were breaking down and confessing their sins. Students who had vowed to each other never to confess were overwhelmed with conviction.

What about the matter of obedience? There are indications in Goforth's book *By My Spirit* that church discipline had been weak. Members and even pastors had slipped far into sin and still were called members. No wonder revival was so necessary in some of the church communities.

We can learn from these people's problems. But even more, we should be challenged by the way these people earnestly repented, diligently sought after God, and put away all known sin. How can we apply these truths to our situation? We all tend to cool off and must be reminded that a little truth on fire can accomplish more than a lot of truth on ice.[7]

What about prominent revivalists of our own times, such as

---

[7] This does not mean that fervency is better than truth but that fervency should be added to truth.

Billy Graham? The same basic principles apply. Obviously these preachers represent such a wide variety of beliefs and degrees of success that we cannot paint them all with the same brush. Some have surely done much better than others.

However, one thing that plagues many modern revivalists is the belief that getting converted is the critical factor in preparing a person to enter glory. Conversion *is* critical, of course. But just as critical is holy living after conversion. In the settings where these men work, there usually is too little emphasis on living a godly life and none at all on belonging to a Biblical, well-disciplined church. Consequently, many "new births" chalked up in such campaigns turn out to be little better than stillbirths.

Now, what about your church and mine? Are you discontent because nothing like a revival ever seems to happen in your church? Maybe the Lord has worked in ways you have not noticed. Since many readers of this book are conservative Mennonites, we will use our own church for an example.

During the 1940s and 1950s, the standards of the Mennonite Church deteriorated steadily, and the old safeguards and expressions of practical obedience were discarded right and left. Many leaders seemed content to ride the popular wave in the wrong direction. But more and more voices rose, warning, protesting, objecting. Finally leaders began to step out and form small dissenting groups. This movement grew to a wave—in the right direction this time—and today conservative-minded people live in many places over North America. Furthermore, they are reaching out to other parts of the world.

This revival involved preaching, but it also involved much more. It included new publishing ventures sponsored by pioneers who were willing to do some things imperfectly just to get the publishing work moving. It involved a new Christian school movement, so sweeping that virtually every child in our groups today receives

Christian teaching rather than going to public school. What is all this but revival?

Moreover, this revival was no mere wave that rose and fell in a few years as many other revivals have done. Rather, it might be compared to an escarpment, which is an ascent that takes travelers from lowlands to highlands. Once at the top, people do not look for the other side of the hill, because they are on a broad plateau. A revival should bring people to higher spiritual ground and give them the resources to stay there—indeed, to go even higher. Today we enjoy high ground because a previous generation prayed and obeyed their way up the escarpment.

But there is another fact that we must consider. No one should rest content with his present standing on the plateau. Neither should he be happy that his church has "made it." Rather, we should all want to reach out. It is a sign of spiritual health to wonder why not more people in the community respond to the pure Gospel. Maybe with more fervent prayer and drawing close to God, it can be done. It is a fascinating idea and one we should not too quickly dismiss.[8]

In the meantime, remember this: many people are already responding. The fact that they come from scattered communities makes this phenomenon seem less dramatic. The fact that they do not all become members in our congregations also makes their response seem less impressive. But many individuals and families are reading Bible-based literature, taking Bible correspondence courses, and making Biblical applications to their own lives. We should not dismiss all this lightly but count it precious. If we want any more revival around us, we must be thankful for what the Lord has already sent and we should contribute to the existing revival

---

[8] Prayer with no object other than revival probably will not work. Prayer with the goal of drawing close to God is already the beginning of revival.

whenever we have opportunity. Further, we must ever press onward, knowing that none of us has already attained or is already perfect.

> Say not, the struggle naught availeth,
>   The labor and the wounds are vain,
> The enemy faints not, nor faileth,
>   And as things have been, they remain.
>
> If hopes were dupes, fears may be liars;
>   It may be, in yon smoke concealed,
> Your comrades chase e'en now the fliers,
>   And, but for you, possess the field.
>
> For while the tired waves, vainly breaking,
>   Seem here no painful inch to gain,
> Far back, through creeks and inlets making,
>   Comes silent, flooding in, the main.
>
> And not by eastern windows only,
>   When daylight comes, comes in the light;
> In front, the sun climbs slow—how slowly!
>   But westward, look, the land is bright!
>   —Arthur Hugh Clough

Chapter Seventeen

What It Means to Be Spiritual

"But ye have obeyed from the heart that form of doctrine which was delivered you" (Romans 6:17).

The apostle Paul once used the expression, "ye which are spiritual" (Galatians 6:1). Evidently, he believed that spiritual people would recognize themselves as such. But no doubt some people wonder what being spiritual really means.

At all-day church meetings, we sometimes see a simple illustration that helps to answer this question. An empty cup sits at each person's place on the lunch table. If the water pitcher is far away, the cup alone does little good. On the other hand, suppose you had no cup and someone came along and poured water anyway. That would not do much good either.

Now learn the parable of the cup and the water. The cup stands for outward disciplines and practical obedience to the Word of God. The water stands for the Holy Spirit and the inner life He brings. Some people tend to emphasize the water at the expense of the cup. They talk about the inner life but neglect things they could do to help preserve that life. Such people are often called pietists (though when speaking of pietists, it is easy to oversimplify). Other people faithfully observe outward religious practices and fail to nurture their spiritual connection to the Lord. Such people are legalists.

Where do we find a balance in this? What is true spirituality? It is having both the cup and the water. It is having "a form of godliness" *and* "the power thereof" (2 Timothy 3:5). It means being careful to follow Bible instructions just as faithfully as one would follow directions in a manual or cookbook. It means belonging to a visible church separate from the world—while also having a deep, warm, inner, personal relationship with the Lord.

How do we promote the outward part of spirituality?

We publicly declare our faith. "That if thou shalt confess with thy mouth the Lord Jesus, and shalt believe in thine heart . . ." (Romans 10:9). This means outward confession, not just inward belief. If we believe secretly and do no more, the vision fades and we end up doubting or rejecting what we once believed.

We obey the Lord's directions. "We are only as spiritual as we are Scriptural." That is a good line to remember when we meet someone who disobeys the Scriptures but seems exceptionally spiritual. "If we live in the Spirit, let us also walk in the Spirit" (Galatians 5:25); that is, God expects us to put our spirituality into shoe leather. "He that saith he abideth in him ought himself also so to walk, even as he walked" (1 John 2:6). Jesus Himself said, "And why call ye me, Lord, Lord, and do not the things which I say?" (Luke 6:46). As a children's song goes, "Obedience is the very best way to show that you believe."[1]

We respect the church's directions. "If any man think himself to be a prophet, or spiritual," wrote Paul, "let him acknowledge that the things that I write unto you are the commandments of the Lord" (1 Corinthians 14:37). Paul was saying, "If you are spiritual, you can take directions from me, an apostle, as if it were from the

---

[1] People who live in the light that God has given them are spiritual, even though they may need growth in understanding some Bible commands.

Lord." No one presently living among us has as much authority as Paul, but some people among us—many people, in fact—have a certain amount of God-given authority. Can the church usher tell you where to sit? Are you spiritual?

We look out for each other's physical welfare. Spiritual men in the early church ordained seven deacons to meet people's practical needs. What those seven deacons did was as necessary for the church as praying. Partly as a result of their labors, "the word of God increased; and the number of the disciples multiplied in Jerusalem greatly" (Acts 6:7). The practical helped the spiritual.

It still does. We do not need to be deacons to see needs and to help people. When someone is ill or a child is born, we usually hear about it. If we can do something to make the present moment a little easier for people, why not do it? Spirituality that has no practical side is simply not spiritual.

We express our concerns verbally. "Brethren, if a man be overtaken in a fault, ye which are spiritual, restore such an one in the spirit of meekness" (Galatians 6:1). It is not enough to pray for and try to have a good attitude toward him. Practical spirituality means you will apply Matthew 18 and talk to the person yourself. Did you say, "I just can't do such a thing"? That could be a measure of your spirituality.

Now let us consider the inner side of spirituality. Earlier we observed the saying, "We are only as spiritual as we are Scriptural." The other side is, "We are no more Scriptural than we are spiritual." The Pharisee who prayed aloud, "I fast twice in the week, I give tithes of all that I possess" (Luke 18:12) was neither spiritual nor Scriptural—not because he did these outward things but because he stopped there.

Jesus told a Samaritan woman, "God is a Spirit: and they that worship him must worship him in spirit and in truth" (John 4:24). We will never make contact with God by merely singing, reading, kneeling, rising, sitting through sermons, wearing certain garments, having fellowship with good people. These things have meaning if a person already knows the Lord. But if he does not, they are worse than useless.

The Samaritan woman to whom Jesus spoke had the idea that the place where people worshiped was important. She was pinning her religiosity on the fact that "our fathers worshipped in this mountain" (John 4:20). Jesus told her that the most important thing is not the place; it is the actual contact between one spirit and another.

How do we promote inner spirituality?

Let us go back to the cup illustration.

We bring our cup to God and admit that it is empty. Doing good deeds, living right, talking right, coming to church—these are all good, but they are outward things. They form the cup; they do not fill the cup. Do not stop doing these things; just stop trusting in them.

We let God cleanse our cup. If you are about to pour pure water into a cup but find a little chocolate milk in it, will you pour? No, you will wash the cup first. God also wants a cup cleansed from sin to pour His Spirit into. He cleanses us through the blood of Jesus.

We cherish and preserve what we already have. "Know ye not that ye are the temple of God, and that the Spirit of God dwelleth in you?" (1 Corinthians 3:16). "Ye are the temple of the living God" (2 Corinthians 6:16). This is present tense. Everyone who is born again has the privilege of having God's Spirit dwell within him, and therefore he is already spiritual in that sense. Praise the Lord for this truth; then move on from there.

We hunger and thirst for more. The person who eats small amounts at irregular times might affect his appetite to the point of ruining it. To encourage our health and appetite, we eat properly. A spiritual person stays spiritual by keeping his soul well-fed, reading and pondering "the sincere milk of the word" (1 Peter 2:2).

It is a mark of spirituality not to be altogether satisfied with our present spiritual attainment. Neither is God. "God is easy to please but hard to satisfy." He wants to see that same attitude reflected in us: "I'm glad for what I have of God, but I want more!"

We abide in Him, and He in us (John 15:4). Not only do we inform ourselves about God, but we also keep Him not too far from our consciousness. We sense His presence, and we enjoy it.

In summary, remember the story of the man wearing religious garb who was told, "There's no religion in your plain coat." The man replied, "When it's hanging on a hook, there's no religion in it. But when I'm wearing it, I believe there is." There is no water in a cup—that is, in the glass or plastic or paper that makes it up. But when someone pours water into it, there is indeed water in the cup.

> All for Jesus, all for Jesus!
> All my being's ransomed pow'rs:
> All my tho'ts and words and doings,
> All my days and all my hours.
> —Mary D. James

Chapter Eighteen

The Holy Spirit's Timetable

"God . . . giveth rain, both the former and the latter, in his season" (Jeremiah 5:24).

On the last dark night before His crucifixion, Jesus told His disciples, "I have yet many things to say unto you, but ye cannot bear them now" (John 16:12). Coming from the Son of God, this is an intriguing statement. God is infinitely powerful, and He could have said everything at once. Did He not speak the universe into existence?

Yes, but when God works with people, He takes His time, just as He did when He made the first man out of dust. This applies to the way He works with individuals as well as with His people in general.

A heartwarming story in Genesis 28 tells how night fell on Jacob when he was traveling alone. For lack of better lodging, he set some stones together for his pillows and slept under the stars. But God knew his lonely location and chose that night to speak to him. "I am with thee; . . . I will not leave thee, until I have done that which I have spoken to thee of" (verse 15).

That memory lingered with Jacob throughout his life. Well it might, for God stood with him just as He had promised. Not that Jacob walked on air for the rest of his life. He had a number of rocky experiences, some unpleasant and some downright harsh. Nevertheless, at the close of life, Jacob described God as "the God which fed me all my life long unto this day" (Genesis 48:15).

Jacob's experience resembles our own. The Lord has promised

in His Word, "I will never leave thee, nor forsake thee" (Hebrews 13:5). The more we study the work of the Holy Spirit, the more we realize this is true. There are no long, blank years when the Spirit is busy elsewhere and leaves us on our own. At each stage of life, He is at our side. "I will not leave thee," is His promise, "until I have done that which I have spoken to thee of."

Before conversion. Even before conversion, we find that the Spirit does not leave us. He has His way among ungodly individuals for reasons of His own. He will not convert them against their will, but He can influence them to do things they did not plan to do. Unknown to them, the Lord is fulfilling His purposes and is leading them to where they can more easily be converted.

The Spirit speaks directly to unconverted hearts. Jesus said of the Spirit, "He will reprove the world of sin, and of righteousness, and of judgment" (John 16:8). Another term for *reprove* might be *convince.* A good example of this is the time Paul gave his testimony before the Roman governor Felix. "And as he reasoned of righteousness, temperance, and judgment to come, Felix trembled" (Acts 24:25). While Paul was speaking to Felix, the Spirit was speaking directly to Felix's heart.

The Holy Spirit was an unwelcome visitor that day, as He is to most hearts when they first hear His call. Nevertheless, that quiet call is the kindest thing the Spirit can give to the lost.

The Holy Spirit's timetable coincides with circumstances. The Spirit does not normally call a person to be a Christian before he has even heard of Christianity. But when he hears or reads the Gospel, then the Spirit does His work. It was when Paul preached to Felix that the Spirit underscored what Paul said and applied it to Felix's own life.

Sometimes even when people hear the Gospel, it does not register with them until the time is right. Children growing up in Christian homes are usually free in conscience at first. But there comes an age when the call of the Spirit becomes increasingly clear. We often refer to this as the age of accountability.

But what age is that? This has long been debated by many Christians. No doubt there is an optimum age, but here again the Spirit works in harmony with His people. Why should He call a child five years before anyone in his congregation expects him to respond? As a rule, He waits until an age considered acceptable in the local church.

Then He calls, and it is up to the youth to respond. Although the Lord's Spirit adjusts His call somewhat to accommodate people, they must also accommodate Him. His call grows ever louder and clearer during the best time for conversion. But then it slowly grows fainter.

With regard to the timing of conversion, we should not try to advance or retard the working of the Spirit. Perhaps the most common danger lies in awaking a child's sense of accountability too soon. It is hardly wise to let a young child read those little paperbacks with stories about small children becoming Christians and with a dotted line on the last page for the child to sign as a way of giving his heart to the Lord. This not only cheapens a child's concept of conversion but also bypasses the maturing process that finally leads a young person to a lifelong commitment.

We can make the same mistake when a young person responds to an invitation to salvation, if we are so elated that we fail to make sure he understands the implications of conversion. A few questions like the following would be in order: "Can you say in your own words why you responded?" "Is there anything in particular that is troubling you just now?" "If we settle this little matter and pray about it, will you be satisfied?"

At the same time, we should beware lest we put off a young person just because he is below a certain age or because he cannot fully express how needy he feels. The Spirit will not look favorably on it if we crush a sense of call that He has carefully been nurturing.

A young person under conviction might make the mistake of comparing himself with another. "When he responds, I will too," he might think. "After all, he's older." Once again, each person must mind the voice of the Spirit in his own heart and let the Spirit call another in His own good time.

At conversion. The Holy Spirit is active when a person is converted. The moment an individual opens his heart's door to the Lord, a new life—the life of God Himself—moves in. "You hath he quickened [made alive]," said Paul in Ephesians 2:1. A death takes place too, to make way for the new life. "Now if we be dead with Christ, we believe that we shall also live with him" (Romans 6:8).

In other words, a transformation takes place. Jesus looked forward to seeing Peter transformed. "When thou art converted," He told Peter in Luke 22:32, "strengthen thy brethren."

The night Jesus was on trial, Peter was frightened by a servant girl. But less than two months later, under the power of the Spirit, he was out of hiding, preaching to thousands. "Ye men of Israel, hear these words," he declared. "Jesus of Nazareth, a man approved of God among you, . . . ye have taken, and by wicked hands have crucified and slain. . . . God hath made that same Jesus, whom ye have crucified, both Lord and Christ" (Acts 2:22, 23, 36).

The Spirit generally does not change people's personalities. If Peter thought that after his conversion he would have a quiet personality like Philip's or Nathanael's, he was mistaken. Peter was outspoken both before and after conversion. The difference was that before conversion he had nothing but himself to back up his words, but afterward he had the Lord's Spirit.

The Spirit that transformed Peter was not just for Peter but for us as well. "Therefore if *any man* be in Christ, he is a new creature: old things are passed away; behold, all things are become new" (2 Corinthians 5:17).

After conversion. Some people think that a conversion experience guarantees a happy ending to life, and that in the meantime they can do as they please. Not so. "The saint who enters heaven, / Who comes of royal birth, / Or dwells with all the sanctified, / Is first a saint on earth."[1] There is no long, dormant period. The time between conversion and death is vitally important.

During this time the Spirit guides a saint heavenward, for the Christian life is not a destination but a journey. The Spirit reassures the child of God with growing conviction that He really does belong to God. He convicts a Christian of new steps he ought to be taking and provides him with new steppingstones. He strengthens a Christian in the struggle against temptation. He intercedes along with a Christian's prayers. Elsewhere in this book, you can read in more detail about a number of things He does.

Here again, we must be careful not to run ahead of the Spirit or fall behind Him. Sometimes we think we should do some great work for the Lord, when all He wants us to do at the moment is peel potatoes (and perhaps sing while we do it). Other times we might wish to retreat into the shadows when the Lord wants us to strike up a conversation with a stranger who has come to church.

Jesus may have struggled in a similar way. He spent long years in obscurity before starting His public ministry. At the age of twelve, He did astonish the Jewish teachers at the temple with His understanding of spiritual things. But as He moved through His twenties, perhaps He wondered why He could not yet strike a public blow for righteousness. On the other hand, sometimes it seemed that things happened too soon. His friends were shocked at His untimely death at the age of thirty-three. Yet all was done with perfect timing. Now His Spirit dwells within us, urging us to keep in step with Him.

Satan tried to throw off Jesus' sense of timing. He offered Jesus all the kingdoms of this world—which He would inherit anyway, but

---

[1] Lewis J. Heatwole, "The Christian's Passport."

not at that moment. Satan still tries to interfere with the Spirit's timing. Constantly he tells people, "It's too early" or "It's too late." But we must remember the old saying, "Strike while the iron is hot." The best time to do anything is while the Spirit is prompting you to do it.

At death. Even fast friends must part at death's door. Does the Spirit also leave us at death? Not at all. When a Christian leaves his body, the Spirit goes along and pilots him through the experience. "Though I walk through the valley of the shadow of death, I will fear no evil: for thou art with me" (Psalm 23:4). When I "meet my Saviour first of all,"[2] I will discover that the Spirit was with me the whole time, guiding me through life and death.

An old man once confided to a friend that he dreaded the thought of dying alone. He had reasons to worry. He was an ungodly man, and without God he was indeed living alone. But if we have already made friends with the Lord and are living with Him, we have His assurance that we will not have to pass alone through the gate of death.

At the final resurrection. The Spirit of God will be present at our resurrection. In fact, He will make it happen. "But if the Spirit of him that raised up Jesus from the dead dwell in you, he that raised up Christ from the dead shall also quicken your mortal bodies by his Spirit that dwelleth in you" (Romans 8:11).

This passage contains two bases for our hope to rise again.

First, God through the power of the Spirit raised up Jesus from the dead. That was no small power. Everyone agreed that Jesus was dead. The attending centurion assured Pilate of the fact. A soldier pierced His side, perhaps to make doubly sure He was dead. Three days in a tomb without any medical attention should remove any lingering doubt. He was not just clinically dead, He was dead. Yet

---

[2]   Fanny J. Crosby, "My Saviour First of All."

He arose, and this verse says that the same power that raised Him up will raise us up too, despite formaldehyde or the lack of it, despite latched casket and concrete vault, and despite six feet of settled earth. *That same power.*

Now the second basis: "If the Spirit . . . dwell in you." Every dead person, good or bad, will be raised in the end whether he desires to be or not. But a happy resurrection to eternal life will take place only if we have had an understanding with the Lord before we die. It will happen only if the Spirit "dwell in you." But if He does dwell in us, it will happen.

In glory. What about our relationship with the Spirit throughout eternity? That is taken for granted! Certainly, we will then have no less of the Spirit than we have now. Remember, the Spirit "is the earnest [down payment] of our inheritance" (Ephesians 1:14). In glory, we will have the down payment plus everything else God has promised us. Just now, through His Spirit, God is present with us while we are not present with Him. How much more will He be present with us, when we *are* present with Him! Finally we will enjoy the full presence of all there is of God—Father, Son, and Holy Ghost.

> Green pastures are before me,
>   Which yet I have not seen;
> Bright skies will soon be o'er me,
>   Where darkest clouds have been.
> My hope I cannot measure,
>   My path to life is free,
> My Saviour has my treasure,
>   And He will walk with me.
> —Anna L. Waring

Chapter Nineteen

Have I Committed
the Unpardonable Sin?

"The waters compassed me about, even to the soul: the depth closed me round about, the weeds were wrapped about my head. I went down to the bottoms of the mountains; the earth with her bars was about me for ever: yet hast thou brought up my life from corruption, O LORD my God" (Jonah 2:5, 6).

For the despairing soul who turned to this chapter first, we have some fast, temporary relief. Have you committed the unpardonable sin, which is sometimes called the sin against the Holy Spirit? Probably not.

We do believe that when Jesus warned about blaspheming against the Holy Spirit, He did it with good reason. The Holy Spirit is not to be trifled with. He is the person of the Trinity who deals directly with humans. If we offend Him to the point that He turns away from us, we lose our link to heaven and cannot possibly be saved. So even though we say that you have probably not committed the unpardonable sin, we are not saying that no matter how deep into sin a person plunges, he can catch himself in the end and somehow arrive in heaven.

Let us see what Jesus said about the unpardonable sin. "And the scribes which came down from Jerusalem said, He hath Beelzebub, and by the prince of the devils casteth he out devils. And he called them unto him, and said unto them in parables, How can Satan cast out Satan? . . . Verily I say unto you, All sins shall be forgiven unto the sons of men, and blasphemies wherewith soever they shall blaspheme: but he that shall blaspheme against the Holy Ghost hath never forgiveness, but is in danger of eternal damnation: because they said, He hath an unclean spirit" (Mark 3:22, 23, 28–30). In Matthew 12:22–32 and Luke 12:10, Jesus gave similar warnings.

It is interesting to observe that in this same context, Jesus' friends were saying, "He is beside himself" (Mark 3:21). Yet Jesus gave His friends no stern warning even though they were seriously wrong. To mistakenly say something incorrect about the Spirit's work is not at all what Jesus was warning about. Neither did He state absolutely that what His opponents had said constituted blasphemy against the Holy Ghost. Some of them might simply have been echoing what others had said without thinking it through.

But there could have been people in the group who were in the process of cutting off all hope for themselves. These were men who had clearly seen the light and had shut their eyes to it. When a mature and responsible person sets his heart absolutely against God, God finally gives him over to a reprobate mind (Romans 1:28). The Spirit turns away from such a person because he has turned away from the Spirit.

Let us also take warning, without going into despair, from certain solemn passages in Hebrews. "For if we sin wilfully after that we have received the knowledge of the truth, there remaineth no more sacrifice for sins, but a certain fearful looking for of judgment and fiery indignation, which shall devour the adversaries. He that despised Moses' law died without mercy under two or three witnesses: of how much sorer punishment, suppose ye, shall he be thought worthy, who hath trodden under foot the Son of God, and hath counted the blood of the covenant, wherewith he was sanctified, an unholy thing, and hath done despite unto the Spirit of grace?" (Hebrews 10:26–29).

The clause "if we sin wilfully" has frightened many people. These words are addressed to Christians who "have received the knowledge of the truth." Now they have sinned, and they must admit they did it on purpose. What hope is there for them?

Once again, we can find some light in the context. The writer of Hebrews, of course, was writing to Hebrews—to Jews who were still finding their way out of the Old Testament economy into New Testament times. He was explaining to them in this chapter that the Old Testament sacrifices had come to an end in God's sight and that the only availing sacrifice for sin was the one Jesus had made on the cross of Calvary. "For it is not possible that the blood of bulls and of goats should take away sins. . . . But this man [Jesus], after he had offered one sacrifice for sins for ever, sat down on the right hand of God. . . . Now where remission of these is, there is no more offering for sin" (Hebrews 10:4, 12, 18).

In essence, the writer was saying, "If you sin deliberately by rejecting Jesus now, where will you turn? You cannot go back to the Old Testament sacrifices, because they are no longer effective. You cannot look forward to some future atonement, because Jesus shed His blood once for all. All you can look forward to is damnation." It is an echo of the same exhortation we find in Hebrews 2:3: "How shall we escape, if we neglect so great salvation?"

Is there any New Testament illustration of someone who sinned willfully and was restored? In 1 Corinthians 5 we read of a man who had become a Christian and was part of the church but was living in adultery. Was he sinning willfully? He certainly was not sinning by accident. Did the apostle Paul then declare his situation hopeless? No. Rather, he directed the church at Corinth to excommunicate that man in the hope that such firm treatment would make him think. Maybe his life could still be turned around (1 Corinthians 5:5). Later the man did repent, and Paul encouraged the Corinthians to forgive him "lest Satan should get an advantage of us: for we are not ignorant of his devices" (2 Corinthians 2:11).

Sometimes individuals are distressed by the passage in Hebrews that says, "For it is impossible for those who were once enlightened, and have tasted of the heavenly gift, and were made partakers of the Holy Ghost, and have tasted the good word of God, and the powers of the world to come, if they shall fall away, to renew them again unto repentance; seeing they crucify to themselves the Son of God afresh, and put him to an open shame. For the earth which drinketh in the rain that cometh oft upon it, and bringeth forth herbs meet for them by whom it is dressed, receiveth blessing from God: but that which beareth thorns and briers is rejected, and is nigh unto cursing; whose end is to be burned" (Hebrews 6:4–8).

What does the expression "fall away" mean? Can a Christian fall without falling away? Apparently he can, for "if any man sin, we have an advocate with the Father, Jesus Christ the righteous: and he is the propitiation for our sins" (1 John 2:1, 2). The Lord provides for our falls so that they need not be the end for us.

There are different kinds of falls, some more serious than others. In the natural world, if a child falls while playing hopscotch, little harm is done. If an adult falls off a stepladder, greater harm might be done, but he will probably not be killed. But if a person falls from high enough to low enough, he will lose his life.

A fall might have more serious consequences than anyone expected, as Ananias and Sapphira discovered (Acts 5:1–11). On the other hand, sometimes it is surprising how far a person can fall and still recover. We should never assume that because a person has had a serious fall, there is no hope for him. We might be happily surprised. By the same token, if we fall, we should not assume there is no hope for us.

This passage in Hebrews sheds light on itself with the words, "It is impossible . . . to renew them again unto repentance." It does not say that God will refuse to forgive no matter how sincerely they repent. It rather indicates that their hearts will be so cold they will not even want to repent. This suggests that if a person is concerned about his spiritual condition and wants to find his way back to the Lord, he has not burned his bridges behind him; he can still repent.

The writer of Hebrews himself, after giving his solemn warnings, hastened to reassure his readers. He wrote, "But, beloved, we are persuaded better things of you, and things that accompany salvation, though we thus speak. For God is not unrighteous to forget your work and labour of love" (Hebrews 6:9, 10).

Concerning a fellow Christian who falls into sin, Menno Simons wrote as follows:

> I would beg and advise all the God-fearing ones, as far as I am able, that if any should revert to the patent works of the flesh, . . . wisely to consider the matter and not to make a mistake in such a case by premature and unseasonable judgment. For the Lord to whom nothing is concealed knows what sin he has committed, whether he has sinned against the Holy Ghost or not. But let them admonish such a one according to the Word of the Lord. If he repents heartily, if he shows true fruits of repentance according to the Scriptures, if he receives a broken, contrite, and penitent heart once more, and a peaceable, joyful, and cheerful mind, then it is manifest that he did not sin against the Holy Ghost.[1]

Despite all reassurances, some supersensitive people will not be reassured. About the time they gain a glimmer of light, they think of some argument against it and down they go again. No criminal ever had a meaner, cleverer prosecutor than they are in condemning themselves. If such you are, and if every time you try to reason yourself out, you fall back in, here are a few things you should know.

---

[1] *The Complete Writings of Menno Simons,* trans. Leonard Verduin, ed. J. C. Wenger (Scottdale, Pa.: Mennonite Publishing House, 1956), p. 565.

The more you resist, the more it persists. This is simple human nature. Try to persuade yourself that you are *not* thirsty, and see what happens. Rather than arguing with yourself or with the devil, see if you can let the matter rest for a time. You can always worry again tomorrow. In the meantime, doubt your doubts a bit. Keep busy; there is usually someone around for whom you can do a favor. Lighten someone else's load, and your own load will become lighter.

You are not alone. Many people have feared that they committed the unpardonable sin, including this writer. So did John Bunyan, author of *The Pilgrim's Progress*. The story of his struggles is perhaps even more comforting than the answer he finally came to, for it helps us realize that other people go through the valley too. After he had fallen and feared he was beyond hope, he was troubled by the passage, "Or profane person, as Esau, who for one morsel of meat sold his birthright. For ye know how that afterward, when he would have inherited the blessing, he was rejected: for he found no place of repentance, though he sought it carefully with tears" (Hebrews 12:16, 17).

Every time Bunyan thought there might be hope for him, back his mind would circle to the thought, "He found no place of repentance, though he sought it carefully with tears." But note the time of Esau's weeping: "when he would have inherited the blessing." The time of the Christian's inheritance is not in this life but in the next! So Esau's tears do not represent the sincere grief of one who repents from sin in this life, but the hopeless weeping of one who misses heaven in the end.

Bunyan made a common mistake: he was afraid to tell anyone about his struggles and so assumed he was alone with his problem. He even feared to pray. Satan told him, "Now to pray is but to add sin to sin; yea, now to pray, seeing God has cast you off, is the next way to anger and offend Him more than you ever did before." Had Bunyan known the many other people who struggled with the same "conviction," he might have seen a pattern in it all and recognized one of Satan's favorite tricks.

Live for the Lord anyway. Bunyan slowly came out into the light, partly through a consoling thought that might help you as well. He decided, "Yet, my case being desperate, I thought with myself I can but die; and if it must be so, it shall once be said, that such an one died at the foot of Christ in prayer. This I did, but with great difficulty, God doth know."

A man known as Brother Lawrence, who lived during the 1600s, came to a similar consoling thought. In a conversation, he shared that "he had long been troubled in mind from a certain belief that he should be damned; that all the men in the world could not have persuaded him to the contrary; but that he had thus reasoned with himself about it: *I engaged in a religious life only for the love of God, and I have endeavored to act only for Him; whatever becomes of me, whether I be lost or saved, I will always continue to act purely for the love of God. I shall have this good at least, that till death I shall have done all that is in me to love Him.*"[2]

This thought did not instantly relieve him of his fears. Indeed, he struggled with his doubts for four years until more light came. But this purpose held him steady through his times of turmoil. It will do the same for you. "Cast not away therefore your confidence, which hath great recompence of reward" (Hebrews 10:35).

> Before the throne my Surety stands,
> My name is written on His hands.
> —*Charles Wesley*

---

[2] Brother Lawrence, *The Practice of the Presence of God*, second conversation. Italics in the original.

Chapter Twenty

The Gifts of the Spirit

"And he gave some, apostles; and some, prophets; and some, evangelists; and some, pastors and teachers" (Ephesians 4:11).

The story of the Corinthians is quite a blessing! Like some of us today, they were immature and had to be told everything. So the apostle Paul did tell them everything, and now we can benefit from his plain, simple instructions.

It seems that the gifts of the Spirit quickly ignited the imagination of the Corinthians. They apparently became unbalanced on this subject, so Paul gave them a well-rounded picture. No other passage in the Bible explains the Spirit's gifts better than 1 Corinthians 12. We will quote only part of it here.

"For to one is given by the Spirit the word of wisdom; to another the word of knowledge by the same Spirit; to another faith by the same Spirit; to another the gifts of healing by the same Spirit; to another the working of miracles; to another prophecy; to another discerning of spirits; to another divers kinds of tongues; to another the interpretation of tongues: but all these worketh that one and the selfsame Spirit, dividing to every man severally as he will. . . . And God hath set some in the church, first apostles, secondarily prophets, thirdly teachers, after that miracles, then gifts of healings, helps, governments, diversities of tongues" (1 Corinthians 12:8–11, 28).

What do we learn from this passage?

Every Christian has some gift, but no one has them all. The "man who has everything" does not exist. Even the apostles, key men that they were, met situations they could not handle alone. When physical and financial needs turned up among the people, they said, "It is not reason that we should leave the word of God, and serve tables" (Acts 6:2). They ordained other men to do the work of deacons, and said, "But we will give ourselves continually to prayer, and to the ministry of the word" (verse 4).

Peter raised Dorcas from the dead; Dorcas could not have raised Peter. Yet Dorcas did things with her needle and thread that Peter could hardly have done. Each person has his own place to fill.

The gifts are the Spirit's property, not ours. Notice in the passage from 1 Corinthians 12 that the Spirit does His own distributing and that He does it alone, "dividing to every man severally as he will." No one tells Him what to do. The Spirit owns the gifts; the person who has the gift is really just a manager of it.

Spiritual gifts give a person a sense of identity. The sensation of being lost in a crowd, even a crowd of friends, can give a person a slight sense of panic. He might think hardly anyone cares if he is present, or would miss him if he were absent. Some people afflicted with this worry end up doing or saying foolish things because subconsciously they think a poor reputation is better than none.

This is all unnecessary. Each person in the church may rest assured that the Spirit knows all about him. He should feel needed because he is needed. He has his own place that no one else can fill.

An excellent illustration of this takes place sometimes after church when people are standing around talking. A small child wraps his arm around what he thinks is his father's knee, only to look up after a while and realize it is the wrong man. The man is not objecting and might even be enjoying this, but the child promptly releases him and turns to his real father. No one else will do.

The father of that child might not have any great talents, but he obviously has an identity. He should realize that other people in the group view him in somewhat the way his children do—that because he is who he is, with whatever gifts he has, large or small, he is loved and wanted. No one else could step in and exactly fill his place—not even an identical twin, if he had one. "There is no indispensable man," truly, but there is no replaceable man either. The Spirit makes sure of that.

Some people must search harder to find their identity than others do. A minister has his identity handed to him. So do people with various talents for whom the church has found offices—for example, the position of trustee. The search for identity becomes more difficult for the ordinary person of average height and build, who got average grades in school and is now an average carpenter or housewife.

The tendency for such people is to lose heart and bury the "one talent" that they do have (it is probably many more than one). They must remember that the Lord is watching them with an interest just as keen as His interest in people with more talents. He takes equal pleasure in His children who scrub kitchen floors as in those who teach Sunday school. "The steps of a good man are ordered by the Lord: and he *delighteth* in his way" (Psalm 37:23).

Church leaders probably understand this concept as well as anyone. They have filled various positions. They know what it is like to preach sermons as well as to wash windows or mow grass, and it is obvious to them (or should be) that God takes satisfaction in both. Other people will simply have to take it by faith.

Spiritual gifts benefit the group, not just the individual. Someone appointed to serve as church librarian should never say, "What's in it for me?" The answer, of course, is, "Nothing. The library is for people who want to check out books to read, and you are there to help them. Your talent for meeting people and keeping things organized is for them, not for you."

What is in it for you if you are called upon to be the mother of five or six children, including a foster child? The same truth applies. The Bible says, "The children ought not to lay up for the parents, but the parents for the children" (2 Corinthians 12:14).

Nevertheless, spiritual gifts do bring the individual much satisfaction. For a good illustration, think of a Sunday school teacher. Most of the gain is for the class; the teacher loses (time and energy) in preparing and teaching the lesson. But he receives much satisfaction as he interacts with the pupils and helps to increase their understanding of the Bible.

Christopher Dock's teaching benefited the children he taught; the schools were not set up to benefit him. Perhaps, financially speaking, he would have been better off farming than teaching school. But he personally became much richer by teaching than by farming, because of the satisfaction it gave him. Dock's only regret in later years was that he had farmed as long as he had.

Diversity of gifts draws the church together. One might think it would work the other way, that people of many different talents would head off in many different directions. Rather, each person sees that he is needed and either steps in or is called by the church to make his contribution. A parallel to the church is the community, where schools, banks, hospitals, stores, factories, utilities, and other agencies all work together. The main difference with the church is that it is the property of the Holy Spirit and works under His management.

Diversity of gifts does not create confusion. The Spirit is directing it all. "Now there are diversities of gifts, but the same Spirit" (1 Corinthians 12:4). The Spirit does not approve when someone leads a little group off on some tangent of his own. That becomes evident when the little following ends up with young people who socially do not fit anywhere and have nowhere to turn. Jesus prayed "that they all may be one" (John 17:21), and His Spirit desires the same today.

Spirituality and the gifts of the Spirit are not always directly proportional. We should not get the idea that because a person has a certain gift, such as the ability to speak well, he is therefore deeply spiritual. No one was physically stronger than Samson when the Spirit of the Lord came mightily upon him. That did not mean he was very spiritual but rather that the Spirit was very forbearing. In fact, Samson was spiritually weak.

The reason God worked with Samson was for the sake of His people in general. God saw that Israel needed Samson's miraculous strength. These days God gives spiritual gifts not as badges or awards but because the church needs the benefit of those gifts. "What hast thou that thou didst not receive? now if thou didst receive it, why dost thou glory, as if thou hadst not received it?" (1 Corinthians 4:7). In other words, why boast as if you had earned the gift?

By the same token, we should not assume that because someone's gifts do not shine the way we think they should, he therefore is not spiritual. John the Baptist did no miracles at all (John 10:41), and Stephen and Philip were the only two deacons of Acts 6 who worked wonders. What about the other five?

Are we saying that being spiritual has nothing to do with the gifts of the Spirit? Of course not. Samson's gift did benefit Israel, but how much more he might have accomplished if he had been truly spiritual! Likewise, when the disciples could not cast out a demon, Jesus explained in effect that they could not because they were not spiritual enough: "Because of your unbelief. . . . This kind goeth not out but by prayer and fasting" (Matthew 17:20, 21). May we have the true inner virtue that enhances the gifts of the Spirit.

We need to keep a proper balance among the gifts. People have a strong tendency to make the least important gift the most important. The gift of tongues looks dramatic and appears to be supernatural, so why not call it the greatest gift? But when the apostle Paul listed spiritual gifts, he put tongues and the interpretation of tongues at the bottom.

Not that Paul despised the gift of tongues. "I speak with tongues more than ye all," he said (1 Corinthians 14:18). He added in verse 22, "Tongues are for a sign . . . to them that believe not." As a sign, the gift of tongues was of considerable value. It had caught people's attention on the day of Pentecost. It had confirmed God's approval when Cornelius and other Gentiles received the Gospel. But the key word in 1 Corinthians 14 is not *sign* but *edification*. That word or one of its forms occurs in verses 3, 4, 5, 12, 17, and 26. So it is not the "sign gifts" but the "gifts for edification" that deserve special emphasis in ongoing church life.

To help keep the gift of tongues in proper proportion to other gifts, Paul gave some specific instructions: (1) Not more than two or three should speak in tongues in any one service (1 Corinthians 14:27). (2) Speakers should take turns (verse 27). (3) If unknown tongues are spoken, someone must interpret (verse 27). (4) If no interpreter is available, no one should speak in tongues (verse 28). He added in the same chapter, "Let your women keep silence in the churches: for it is not permitted unto them to speak" (verse 34). And, "Let all things be done decently and in order" (verse 40). When all these safeguards are followed, it is safe to say, "Forbid not to speak with tongues" (verse 39).

Some gifts of the Spirit are not on the "official list." The list that Paul wrote gives a sample of the gifts, not a complete inventory. Other gifts he could have mentioned are the ability to bring people of diverse views together, the ability to summarize and express ideas, the ability to write well, and the ability to make a house a home. He could also have mentioned that some people have a gift for appreciating other people's gifts and inspiring them to keep making their contribution. Talented people are not always confident people, and they need a quiet word of encouragement now and then.

We should not despise our own particular gift. After all, it is a gift! If someone gives you a gift, he is pleased to see you pleased. If the gift is gloves, the giver wants to see you smile and put them on. God is pleased in the same way to see you exercising your gifts and enjoying the privilege.

People tend to despise whatever gift they have, just as they often despise the color of their hair and even try to change it. Do not do that with your gift. Treasure it. Take care of it. Do not disdain your gift just because it is yours.

Gifts need to be developed. No one should expect a young man to have a fully developed gift for preaching the first time he stands up to speak. It takes development, not only of ability but also of the depth that comes only with experience. We are back to the concept that God can do things instantly by just speaking the word; but when He deals with people, He goes more slowly. He works at a pace that limits the temptation to become lifted up with pride. Since God is so patient, the least we can do is be patient too and cooperate with Him.

The gifts are given to advance the fruit. After Paul wrote, "Covet earnestly the best gifts," he added, "and yet shew I unto you a more excellent way" (1 Corinthians 12:31). That "more excellent way," as we see in 1 Corinthians 13, is love—one part of the fruit of the Spirit.

So easily we hold the gifts of the Spirit in higher esteem than the fruit of the Spirit. But God's reason for giving the gifts is to make people more spiritually fruitful. Usually a minister does not preach about the gift of preaching, but about the inner virtues God wants us to have—the fruit of the Spirit. The disciples who spoke in tongues on the day of Pentecost did not preach about how to get the gift of tongues; they proclaimed the wonderful works of God.

Always we must keep first things first. Jesus emphasized this when the disciples rejoiced and said, "Lord, even the devils are subject unto us through thy name." He acknowledged this but replied, "Notwithstanding in this rejoice not, that the spirits are subject unto you; but rather rejoice, because your names are written in heaven" (Luke 10:17, 20). Today He would say, "Rejoice not so much because you can write poetry or put much money in the offering, but rather rejoice because these things can help people to bear more of the fruit of the Spirit."

The glory and pleasure go to God. Everyone benefits by the arrangement we have described, but the greatest satisfaction goes to the One who planned it all. No doubt a city planner smiles when he flies over a city and sees the many paved arteries streaming with traffic, everything working smoothly together. Does the Lord get any less satisfaction when He looks upon the church?

Incidentally, when we arrive in glory, we need not be surprised if some arrangements look familiar. We will all be more complete than we are now, but quite likely we will still be interdependent, still making each other more complete by our unique contributions, still drawing each other into the great plan, still pleasing the Lord, who designed it all.

> Shamgar had an oxgoad,
>   David had a sling,
> Dorcas had a needle,
>   Rahab had a string,
> Samson had a jawbone,
>   Aaron had a rod,
> Mary had some ointment,
>   But they all were used for God.

Chapter Twenty-one

The Fruit of the Spirit

*"For a good tree bringeth not forth corrupt fruit; nei-
ther doth a corrupt tree bring forth good fruit" (Luke 6:43).*

Those colorful seed catalogs make a gardener's mouth water.
Crisp lettuce, plump tomatoes, juicy-looking berries of all sorts!
Of course, the advertisers could have included pictures showing
the means by which to produce the fruit. They could have shown
hoes, rakes, garden hoses, and bags of fertilizer. But they kept those
items in the background in order to focus on the fruit, which is
much more appealing (and more likely to induce you to buy).

The apostle Paul could have lingered longer on the subject of
the gifts of the Spirit in 1 Corinthians 12, but he moved on to a
more important subject: "And yet shew I unto you a more excellent way." In the next chapter, he talked about love. As he wrote,
he was exercising a spiritual gift—the ability to organize and express
his thoughts—but he did not mention that. He was focusing on love,
a major part of the fruit of the Spirit (Galatians 5:22, 23).

The fruit of the Spirit provides more solid evidence of spiritual
life than the gifts do. Jesus did not say, "Ye shall know them by
their gifts," but "Ye shall know them by their fruits" (Matthew
7:16). People can more easily imitate the gifts than the fruit. Gifts
of healing, prophecy, discerning of spirits, tongues—these can be
mimicked, and some people even make merchandise of their supposed gifts. But live with them, and observe how well they show

the fruit—the love, long-suffering, gentleness, meekness, temperance. *That* is the real test.

People do also imitate the fruit of the Spirit. Some unbelievers have polished their social skills to the point that they shine more than some Christians do. But the glow is often mainly for public display, and the Lord knows the whole story. Not that a fine appearance is wrong, but the quality must go deeper than the surface. A bowl of plastic fruit might look prettier than a bowl of real fruit, but no one hesitates over the choice when he is hungry for a juicy apple.

Looking more closely at the fruit of the Spirit, we notice again the old principle. What the Spirit is, Jesus was while on earth. All His life, He was a model of love, joy, peace, long-suffering, gentleness, goodness, faith, meekness, and temperance. Now He wants to live out those same virtues in His children.

Jesus was a model of *love,* perfectly unselfish and concerned for the good of others. He still loves people, showing it by the unselfishness and concern of God's children, in whose hearts He dwells.

Did Jesus have *joy*? Jesus, the "man of sorrows"? We know that He had a joy "set before him," toward which He moved. What about during His earthly life in the meantime? Yes, He "rejoiced in spirit" (Luke 10:21). Joy is the sense that the most important things in our life are all right even if the moment seems all wrong. We serve a joyful Lord—joyful because the most important things in His universe are in order. And His joy keeps welling up in us, making each day a little brighter and its load a little lighter. Even when we grieve, we "sorrow not, even as others which have no hope" (1 Thessalonians 4:13).

Jesus was also a man of *peace,* at peace with Himself and with His Father. He was and is eager to make peace even with His enemies. As victor over all challengers, He can afford to be generous.

We too, having peace with the Lord and being on the winning side, can afford to be generous with those who want to take advantage of us. Perhaps we can motivate them to find peace with the Prince of Peace.

Without any question, Jesus was *long-suffering*. His disciples could recount story after story along this line, some to their own embarrassment. They even included a few of these accounts in the Gospels, such as the times they disputed among themselves about who should be the greatest. But Jesus could see beyond their present, irritating childishness, and He told them, "Ye . . . shall sit upon twelve thrones, judging the twelve tribes of Israel" (Matthew 19:28). Now His farseeing, patient Spirit resides in us, enabling us to see the big picture and helping us also to be patient with people.

Was Jesus *gentle*? He did not hesitate to speak a hard-hitting truth to someone if He thought plain speech might wake him up. But gentleness was His trademark because that was how He could reach the most people. Today His Spirit is so gentle that people easily shrug Him off. Yet His very gentleness, represented by His gentle children, draws people back to Him. "Get off my property," snarls the man of the house to someone who offers him a tract, "and don't come back, and tell your people I said so!" "Have a good day, sir!" comes the reply. The incident might bear fruit sometime.

Goodness seemed like a natural trait for Jesus, who "went about doing good" (Acts 10:38). Naturally, He desires the same trait for His people. "Love . . . bless . . . do good . . . pray," He instructed us, "that ye may be the children of your Father which is in heaven: for he maketh his sun to rise on the evil and on the good, and sendeth rain on the just and on the unjust" (Matthew 5:44, 45). This kind of goodness is more than "God rubbing off on us"; it is God living His life in us through His Spirit.

Jesus had great *faith* in His unseen Father, if we can call it faith. He knew without a doubt. And today the Spirit knows His own strength and wonders at our lack of faith! But faith is only half of the story; the other half is *faithfulness*—an aspect always included in the Greek word *pistis*. Jesus is "a merciful and faithful high priest" (Hebrews 2:17), and we live "by the faith [or faithfulness] of the Son of God" (Galatians 2:20). What spiritual fruit is more refreshing than faithfulness and consistency in the lives of Christians?

No one was a better example of *meekness* than Jesus at Calvary. When they took away His coat, He let them have His cloak also. He prayed for those who despitefully used and persecuted Him. He never drew a line in the sand and dared people to cross it. Today His Spirit is meek within believers even in the injustices of the twenty-first century (such as public bias against Christian beliefs). He knows for a fact that He will finally inherit the earth. Through the meek testimony of His people, He desires to draw others so that they too can share in His inheritance.

And what about *temperance*? Jesus was accused of being "a gluttonous man, and a winebibber" (Luke 7:34), but He kept on eating and drinking with publicans and sinners. He had Himself under control and was confident of that. He not only calls His children to be self-controlled but to be under the control of His Spirit— the most balanced and controlled influence there ever was. The Spirit does not make sensible people excessive or lopsided; He calls them back toward center and gives them a sense of balance. Spirit-filled people are confident of this no matter what others say about them.

Fruit is a gift. Nothing the owner of an apple tree can do will earn the shining fruit that finally hangs on his tree. Indeed, an apple is not only a gift but a miracle. No one yet has built an apple factory, for an edible apple is absolutely beyond imitation.

At the same time, producing fruit takes personal nurture. If you hold an apple in your hand, it is because someone planted an apple tree. He had to be patient for years before it began to bear. Possibly he protected the tree from various pests. He may have had to water it. Finally the apple had to be picked, preserved, and transported. Yes, the apple is a gift from God, but it also represents human effort, labor, and commitment. The fruit of a tree takes work!

The fruit of the Spirit is like apples. It is a gift and a miracle, and it cannot be produced by thinking, deciding, attempting, resolving, willing, straining, or any such thing. "For by grace [God's, not yours] are ye saved through faith; and [even that is] not of yourselves: it is the gift of God: not of works, lest any man should boast" (Ephesians 2:8, 9).

At the same time, the fruit of the Spirit does not grow without our care. "If we live in the Spirit, let us also walk in the Spirit" (Galatians 5:25). Although only God can supply that life in the Spirit, we must do the walking.

The fruit of the Spirit takes time to mature. In a measure, we have the fruit of the Spirit from the day of conversion. But then the Lord brings us through various experiences that make us more fruitful. We realize that here or there is a fallow area in our lives that the Lord would like to break up and cultivate. Perhaps we have been wasting our time or energy on something trivial, or spending our money for that which is not bread. Perhaps without realizing it, we have been reserving a corner of our lives for ourselves, such as a pet attitude that is not quite right.

The Lord continues to work with us, often through experiences that reveal the weak points in our lives. Then, as we realize our needs and turn them over to Him, He can make us more loving, more joyful, more fruitful in every way. This process will continue all our lives. In the process, let us not pray, as someone is said to have done, "Lord, give me patience, and I want it right now."

We need not stop with the fruit listed in Galatians 5. Paul did not mean to limit us to this list, neither would he have objected to Peter's list in 2 Peter 1:5–7 (faith, virtue, knowledge, temperance, patience, brotherly kindness, charity). This is just a fair sample of what the Spirit of our Lord does in our lives.

We often say, "Only what's done for Christ will last." That is true, but a better way of saying it might be, "Only what Christ does in us will last." Considering who He is, that is no small amount, and its effects will last into eternity.

> As rays of light from yonder sun,
> The flow'rs of earth set free,
> So life and light and love came forth
> From Christ living in me.
> —*D. W. Whittle*

Chapter Twenty-two

The Holy Spirit
in Figures of Speech

"I have . . . used similitudes" (Hosea 12:10).

It is always difficult to picture the Holy Spirit, and with good reason: spirits cannot be pictured. Sometimes when we hand a photograph of a loved one to a friend, we say, "It misses so much." How can we show in a flat photograph the spirit of a person—something about his or her attitude, loving manner, enthusiasm, or whatever it is? We end up saying, "I wish you could have met him."

Still, a photograph is better than nothing. And the figures of speech God gave us in the Bible help us to understand the Holy Spirit better than if we had no word pictures at all.

Sometimes a Bible writer admitted that the comparison he used did not do justice to what he was trying to describe. Ezekiel, in describing his visions, wrote of "the appearance of fire," rather than just "fire" (Ezekiel 1:27). Luke in Acts 2 wrote of "a sound from heaven as of a rushing mighty wind" and "cloven tongues like as of fire." That cautious little word *as* tells us that the Spirit transcended wind and fire as we know them. Sometimes, of course, Bible writers said things like "our God is a consuming fire" (Hebrews 12:29). They assumed we would know that the fire of God has a much greater power and intensity than the crackling yellow fire in a fireplace.

Sometimes if we are not satisfied that a photograph does justice to a friend, we try to help the situation by bringing out more photographs. Seeing the person in various settings and from different angles helps to give a better understanding. So also in learning about the Spirit, we have been given more than one word picture of Him, and that helps us to understand. He is not only a wind but a fire. He is not just oil but wine. We will look at a number of these pictures now.

Wind

"The wind bloweth where it listeth," Jesus told Nicodemus, "and thou hearest the sound thereof, but canst not tell whence it cometh, and whither it goeth: so is every one that is born of the Spirit" (John 3:8). He seemed disappointed when Nicodemus replied, "How can these things be?" He had given the illustration to make His concept easier, not harder.

How is wind like the Spirit? Neither wind nor the Spirit can be controlled by man. "The wind bloweth where it listeth," and we cannot change that fact. Neither can we harness the Holy Spirit for our own purposes at the moment. Some of us have wished we could speak in tongues at least a little when we were trying to converse with a friend from a foreign country, but the Spirit did not give us that gift. It is His choice, not ours.

So then we must put ourselves at the Spirit's disposal rather than the other way around. We must live right and thus place ourselves where the blessings are, rather than trying to invoke God's blessings on the life of our choosing. The Spirit will have His way in the end, so we will be happier if we let Him have His way all along.

Fire

Fire is no power to play with. Communities have fire departments because everyone understands that once a fire starts roaring, it becomes a power extremely hard to deal with. In fact, men who fight forest fires will tell you that in certain cases all you can do is run.

God speaks of fire as a symbol of Himself. He even had what we call His prophet of fire, Elijah. This man called fire from heaven more than once (1 Kings 18; 2 Kings 1), and a chariot of fire appeared just before he was caught up into heaven (2 Kings 2). Daniel saw a vision of the Ancient of Days, whose "throne was like the fiery flame, and his wheels as burning fire. A fiery stream issued and came forth from before him" (Daniel 7:9, 10). And Isaiah spoke of "devouring fire" (Isaiah 33:14).

God had His prophet of fire in the New Testament too—Jesus Christ Himself. John the Baptist said of Him, "He shall baptize you with the Holy Ghost and with fire" (Luke 3:16). Jesus said of Himself, "I am come to send fire on the earth" (Luke 12:49).

God can do something with fire that we cannot do. We must always let fire destroy something in order to keep it burning. But when God showed Himself to Moses in a desert bush, "the bush burned with fire, and the bush was not consumed" (Exodus 3:2). This was not "everlasting destruction" like the fires of hell, nor was it like the last great day when "the heavens being on fire shall be dissolved, and the elements shall melt with fervent heat" (2 Peter 3:12). The fire Moses saw was like the fire we enjoy today, a gracious fire that warms, comforts, and inspires.

God's fire is precious to Him, and He fans it wherever He finds it. It was prophesied of Jesus, "The smoking flax shall he not quench" (Isaiah 42:3). Wherever He found the tiniest evidence of fire in people's hearts, He encouraged it. "Thou art not far from the kingdom of God," He told a thinking scribe in Mark 12:34. And to a dying thief who said, "Lord, remember me when thou comest into thy kingdom," He replied, "To day shalt thou be with me in paradise" (Luke 23:42, 43). Not surprisingly, the people among us who have the most Spirit fire are the most eager to see other people catching fire too. Every little evidence of fire they see, they rejoice over and encourage.

Can Spirit fire be imitated? Can people imagine the fire present when really it is absent? It happens all the time. God pleaded with such people, calling them "ye that . . . compass yourselves about with sparks" (Isaiah 50:11). Bright smiles and fervent testimonies may or may not be evidence of the Spirit's fire. What God calls fire is fire. Anything else is mere sparks.

By the same token, Spirit fire might be thought missing when really it is still there. Most Christians have days when they run out of everything that looks like fire. Their energy runs low, their spirits sag, and they wonder where the Holy Spirit is. Such Christians need to know that to run out of steam is not the same as to run out of fire. With a little rest and refreshment, they will soon be active in the Lord's service again.

Oil

Sometimes oil in Bible stories represented consecration and apparently no more. Jacob at Bethel anointed a pillar to represent the deep religious experience he had had there. Moses anointed the tabernacle in Leviticus 8:10 as a way of consecrating it.

Sometimes it appears that oil represented consecration and something more besides. When Samuel anointed Saul king, the Spirit came on Saul the same day (1 Samuel 10:1, 6, 9). When David was anointed king, "the Spirit of the LORD came upon David from that day forward" (1 Samuel 16:13). The Spirit gave these men something of God to help them do God's work more effectively. The oil represented the enabling touch of the Holy Spirit.

The Bible calls for anointing people with oil who are seriously or chronically ill (James 5:14, 15). This seems to represent a seeking after what only God can do when the patient senses that ordinary medicines and treatments are not enough. "The Lord shall raise him up" needs its proper emphasis—not necessarily "The Lord *shall* raise him up," but "*The Lord* shall raise him up" when no one else can. Here again, we must let the Spirit have His way.

By applying the oil, we are not trying to force His hand but rather we are letting the Great Physician do what He sees best. The oil represents the healing touch of the Holy Spirit.

The Old Testament priests needed oil constantly. With it, they fed the seven-branched candlestick, the source of light for the tabernacle (Exodus 27:20, 21). The hymn writer caught the meaning of this when he wrote, "Holy light doth fill this place, / Spirit light our way to guide; / In the presence of Thy face / Sin and darkness ne'er can hide."[1] The festival of Hanukkah (Feast of Lights) celebrates a time when the Jews had only enough oil to feed the candlestick for one day. Miraculously, the oil kept the lights burning for eight days. Evidently God was as eager to keep the light burning as they were.

Jesus was that light in His time. He warned the Jews, "Yet a little while is the light with you. Walk while ye have the light, lest darkness come upon you" (John 12:35). But privately to His disciples, He promised a light that would continue with them long after He was gone. "I am the light of the world" did not become obsolete when Jesus left. "He that followeth me shall not walk in darkness, but shall have the light of life" (John 8:12). This is as true now as it ever was, for the Spirit of Christ now lights the souls of men. John wrote, "But the anointing which ye have received of him abideth in you, and ye need not that any man teach you: but as the same anointing teacheth you of all things, and is truth, and is no lie, and even as it hath taught you, ye shall abide in him" (1 John 2:27). This anointing is the enlightening of the Holy Spirit.

In connection with that, however, Jesus gave a solemn warning. He told of ten virgins who went forth to meet the bridegroom, five of whom failed to keep their lamps supplied with oil. At the critical moment, they awoke to the fact that they did not have enough. Some of us—probably all of us—tend to think that because the fires are burning at the present, they always will burn. We can fall back

---

[1]   Samuel F. Coffman, "In Thy Holy Place We Bow."

into the easiest and laziest way of keeping things looking good. We could wake up at a critical moment only to realize that what we did was not enough. "Watch therefore," said Jesus (Matthew 25:13).

Wine

On the day of Pentecost, curious crowds heard the disciples speaking in various languages. Some mocked them and said, "These men are full of new wine" (Acts 2:13). That was the quickest explanation they could think of. They were wrong, but in some ways the Spirit does resemble wine.

Wine makes people do unusual things, things hard to explain. The Spirit certainly was doing that to His people at Pentecost. Every man who cared to could hear the Gospel in his native language. But evidently if he listened for other languages, he could hear them too and laugh at what he could not understand. Men still do that, shaking their heads over a Christian's unconventional way of thinking and talking.

Wine takes control. When a person is full of wine, he is not full up to the neck, but he is fully under the control of wine. The Spirit takes control of people too, but with one great difference. Whereas wine takes away people's power to think rationally, the Spirit never controls people without their permission. He operates on a moment-by-moment basis, only with full cooperation. He makes no slaves and no addicts. It is a high compliment to the Spirit that so many people willingly come under His control. Obviously, they like every minute of it and want more of the same.

Wine is said to be the answer to every problem. If you are hot, a drink of wine will cool you off. If you are cold, a drink will warm you up. If you are sick, a drink will make you feel better. If you are healthy, a drink will help keep you in shape. If you win some triumph, you need a drink to celebrate. If you lose, you need a drink to cheer you up.

Wine, of course, disappoints the user. Jesus is the true One to whom we can turn in any situation. "Is any among you afflicted? let him pray. Is any merry? let him sing psalms. Is any sick among you? let him call for the elders of the church" (James 5:13, 14). Whether "the sun of bliss is beaming" or "the woes of life o'ertake me,"[2] He is the wine for every situation.

Although there are some similarities between wine and the Spirit, the New Testament suggests that they are mutually exclusive. It was said of John the Baptist, "He . . . shall drink neither wine nor strong drink; and he shall be filled with the Holy Ghost, even from his mother's womb" (Luke 1:15). Again the Bible says, "Be not drunk with wine, wherein is excess; but be filled with the Spirit" (Ephesians 5:18). That is natural. Very few people want both kinds of wine anyway. If they are under the influence of wine, they do not want the Spirit. But if they have the Spirit, they think, "Who needs wine when he can have the real thing?"

Bread

"I am the living bread which came down from heaven," Jesus said. He added, "He that eateth me, even he shall live by me" (John 6:51, 57).

Jesus had just fed five thousand men, and some of them had sought Him out again the next day. Of course, He knew what they wanted. He told them, "Ye seek me, not because ye saw the miracles, but because ye did eat of the loaves, and were filled. Labour not for the meat which perisheth, but for that meat which endureth unto everlasting life, which the Son of man shall give unto you: for him hath God the Father sealed" (John 6:26, 27). They had a natural hunger, but Jesus was pointing out their spiritual hunger.

These people, like little children, were slow to catch on. As we know, little children have not learned to recognize all their own body signals and might need to be fed or put to bed before they

---

2   John Bowring, "In the Cross of Christ I Glory."

know why they are grouchy. These people had learned to recognize natural hunger when their stomachs rumbled, but they had not learned to recognize hunger of the spirit.

In case anyone misunderstood, Jesus clarified His words. "It is the spirit that quickeneth; the flesh profiteth nothing: the words that I speak unto you, they are spirit, and they are life" (John 6:63). What was He saying? Simply that by giving Himself to the people—that is, by giving His Spirit—He could fill the vacancy within them that He was trying to help them recognize.

Today we hear that "people are overfed and undernourished." Never is this more true than in the spiritual realm. People stuff their lives with—well, with stuff—possessions, activities, all kinds of things. They cannot understand how those of us who love the Lord manage to get along without all those empty calories.

The people of Jesus' day did not realize they were already observing a holiday that pointed forward to the coming of the Holy Spirit. Just after the Passover, they had waved a sheaf of grain before the Lord in gratitude for the harvest first fruits. Seven weeks later, they observed Pentecost, a festival called by various names in the Old Testament. On that day they waved two loaves of bread before the Lord in gratitude for the harvest (Leviticus 23:15–17). The bread stood for the final results of all the Lord had done for them. The people did not know that Jesus would die on the Passover, rise on the Day of First Fruits, and come again in the Spirit at Pentecost, the day of celebration for a full harvest.

On the day of Pentecost, the Lord had *His* harvest, for "the same day there were added unto them about three thousand souls" (Acts 2:41).

Water

The Jews' Feast of Tabernacles was a happy time. One of its highlights was a ritual that was observed each morning when a golden pitcher was brought from the pool of Siloam to the temple.

There the high priest would ceremoniously pour out the water while trumpets sounded and the people shouted.

Imagine how all this looked to Jesus as He observed the empty, arid lives of many of the participants. No wonder that "in the last day, that great day of the feast, Jesus stood and cried, saying, If any man thirst, let him come unto me, and drink. He that believeth on me, as the scripture hath said, out of his belly shall flow rivers of living water" (John 7:37, 38). This, of course, was a spiritual offer, as the following verse makes clear: "(But this spake he of the Spirit, which they that believe on him should receive)."

This was not the first time Jesus had compared the Spirit to water. To the Samaritan woman at Jacob's well, He had promised, "Whosoever drinketh of this water shall thirst again: but whosoever drinketh of the water that I shall give him shall never thirst; but the water that I shall give him shall be in him a well of water springing up into everlasting life" (John 4:13, 14).

What lesson does this translate into for everyday life? Much the same lesson as we learn from spiritual bread, a lesson that bears repeating. The Lord offers satisfaction that flows from the inside out rather than from the outside in. It is a permanent satisfaction rather than the type of pleasure that leaves us thirsting again in half a day.

We can make a few more analogies. A good drink of water generally comes from a low source—a stream or well. We humble ourselves to get a good drink. By the same token, we kneel to pray. We fast to bring ourselves low. We accept our own mistakes as messengers to remind us how human we are. Failing in this, we can find ourselves dry just because we insisted on staying too high.

We learn the same lesson from the verse that tells us we "have been all made to drink into one Spirit" (1 Corinthians 12:13). That puts all who love the Lord on the same level. Of course, we have much in common with all men, good or bad, for God "hath made of one blood all nations of men" (Acts 17:26). But the water of the

Spirit gives us something that only saints share and that all saints share together. In this case, water is thicker than blood.

When the legendary King Arthur conferred with his knights, they sat at a round table, symbolizing that every man was as good as any other man. The Lord chose a different symbolism that means basically the same thing. We share one common Spirit whom all may drink into and who is as good in one saint as in another.

The Heavenly Dove

Some weeks ago, our family visited a pet shop. A bird like a small parrot rode around on the saleslady's shoulder. Someone started to reach out a friendly hand to the bird, but the lady warned, "He bites."

How different from a dove. Many of us are familiar with the melancholy "coo-aah! coo, coo, coo" of mourning doves on quiet summer mornings. It is a peaceful sound. The appearance of a dove, graceful but subdued in color, adds to that impression.

When Jesus was baptized, the Spirit descended from heaven in the form of a dove and rested on Him (Mark 1:9–11). This did not fit the mental picture many people of that time had of their Messiah. Surely, they thought, He would lead His people to overthrow the oppressive Romans. Rather than a dove, why should not a crown descend, or at least a conqueror's olive wreath? But it was not yet time for Christ to be "the Lion of the tribe of Juda" (Revelation 5:5). He had a lamblike spirit, a dovelike spirit. He said, "The Son of man is not come to destroy men's lives, but to save them" (Luke 9:56).

The people of His day, including His own disciples, should have been glad of this for their own sakes. And we can be thankful for our sakes that the dove is still presiding today. "Gently and long did He plead with my soul,"[3] we sing. Suppose He had not? After all, no one obliged Him to be gentle with us. But He was and still

---

3　"Seeking for Me."

is, for He still brings "light and comfort from above."[4]

Today the Spirit rests on us and makes us "harmless as doves" (Matthew 10:16)—a trait that grows out of peace within. Our neighbors should notice this; then some of them may be influenced to make a home for that dove in their own hearts.

> Spirit of power,
> Spirit of God,
> Spirit of burning,
> Work through Thy Word;
> Search us and sift us,
> Spare not the dross,
> Show us that self-life
> Ends at the cross.
> —*D. W. Whittle*

---

4   Simon Browne, "Come Gracious Spirit, Heavenly Dove."

Chapter Twenty-three

The Comforter

"Jesus himself drew near, and went with them" (Luke 24:15).

After Jesus fed the five thousand on a lonely shore of Galilee, He sent everyone away and disappeared into the mountains. Evening was falling. His disciples went to the shore without Him, took a boat, and headed for home. They had to row—no sailing this time—because the wind was blowing the wrong direction. Poignantly John writes, "And it was now dark, and Jesus was not come to them" (John 6:17).

We can imagine how they felt. Without Jesus on such a tedious, sleepless night, the darkness seemed cheerless and the boat seemed empty. Then to make matters worse, a strange apparition came slowly toward them. It appeared that a man was performing the impossible feat of walking on water. The disciples knew that demons roamed the earth (Luke 11:24), and it was no idle statement when some of them cried out, "It is a spirit!" (Matthew 14:26). How they must have wished Jesus were with them!

But then came the familiar voice: "It is I; be not afraid." Can we imagine how their hearts leaped for joy? Everything was all right again, for the stranger on the sea was Jesus Himself.

After the disciples took Him into the ship, a miracle took place. "And immediately the ship was at the land whither they went" (John 6:21). Jesus solved their problems of the night by bringing the ship to shore. This miracle, however, is mentioned in only one of the four Gospels, and even John mentions it only in passing. The thing that seemed to impress the disciples most was not that Jesus had solved their problems. It was simply that He was present.

There were other times too when the disciples were happy to see Jesus arrive. Once when He was absent, they tried to cast a particularly stubborn demon out of a youth. We know the mortification they must have felt, standing over a sufferer and commanding the demon to leave, only to see his bizarre behavior continue. This was no secret failure either, for when Jesus arrived, "he saw a great multitude about them, and the scribes questioning with them" (Mark 9:14).

It remained for Jesus to say, "Thou dumb and deaf spirit, I charge thee, come out of him, and enter no more into him" (verse 25). We can only imagine the disciples' relief. But they were relieved even before the evil spirit was cast out. The Master had come. He was taking charge.

Later Jesus left His disciples for a few days when they desperately wanted Him to be present. Indeed, His absence was the cause of their desperation. Jesus had known it would be this way and had tried to prepare them beforehand. "I go away, and come again unto you" (John 14:28). "Ye shall weep and lament, but the world shall rejoice: and ye shall be sorrowful, but your sorrow shall be turned into joy" (John 16:20). No words, however, could altogether prepare them for the shock when Jesus was crucified. Other men buried Jesus while the shattered disciples wept.

A few days later, the risen Jesus reappeared to His disciples. In one of the Bible's great understatements, John wrote, "Then were the disciples glad, when they saw the Lord" (John 20:20). They had tried to console each other by huddling together and talking, but no human words could compare with this. Either the Lord was there or He was not—and He was there.

A few weeks later, when Jesus rose into a cloud, the disciples felt the loss again. As we would have done, they craned their necks and strained their eyes for a last glimpse of the One who had comforted them so long.

But they remembered something. The same night Jesus had promised to come back to them after His crucifixion, He had also promised that He would come to them after His ascension. "And I will pray the Father, and he shall give you another Comforter, that he may abide with you for ever; even the Spirit of truth; . . . ye know him; for he dwelleth with you, and shall be in you" (John 14:16, 17). Again He said, "It is expedient for you that I go away: for if I go not away, the Comforter will not come unto you; but if I depart, I will send him unto you" (John 16:7).

Indeed, Jesus seemed to be saying that the Comforter would give better comfort than He was able to provide in the flesh, which was no small comfort. The Comforter is much more than a "consolation prize" to pacify us while the real Jesus is absent. "*I* will not leave you comfortless," Jesus said. "*I* will come to you" (John 14:18). Now He is without the limits imposed on Him when He was here in the flesh. Now He is present with every believer everywhere, and no one ever again need row across the Sea of Galilee without Him.

Of course, the Comforter is no substitute for human companionship. It is said that when a certain boy was afraid to sleep alone, his mother sought to comfort him by saying, "You know God is with you all the time." He replied, "Yes, but I want someone I can touch." Christians can be lonely in the same way.

At the same time, human companionship is no substitute for the Comforter. No loneliness runs so deep as the loneliness of someone in a crowd, without God. The Spirit fills a place no other can fill; indeed He fills a place all others together cannot fill. This thought so inspired the psalmist that he burst out with "Whom have I in heaven but thee? and there is none upon earth that I desire beside thee" (Psalm 73:25).

We see in all of this one of the greatest comforts of the Comforter. Before He ever does anything in our lives, He simply comes in and abides with us. He comes to *do* but first of all just to *be* there. He fulfills the promise, "I will come in to him, and will sup with him, and he with me" (Revelation 3:20).

The idea of the Holy Spirit's comfort is found in various places in the New Testament. We read of "walking in the fear of the Lord, and in the comfort of the Holy Ghost" (Acts 9:31). "The grace of the Lord Jesus Christ, and the love of God, and the communion of the Holy Ghost, be with you all" (2 Corinthians 13:14). Communion is fellowship, such as we enjoy after church or in each other's homes. "Where two or three are gathered together in my name," Jesus said, "there am I in the midst of them" (Matthew 18:20). Gatherings of believers have their social comforts, but most comforting of all is the Lord's presence with them.

What kinds of comfort does the Comforter bring to us?

The comfort of the assurance that we belong to God. When a child gets lost in a shopping mall, one of the most frightening things is that he can see nothing to belong to. Everything looks big and strange and scary. Let him catch one glimpse of his father, and he cheers up considerably. Once again, he belongs.

God knows that we, His children, feel the same way. "Is my name written there?"[1] we sing, and we like to conclude with "Yes, my name's written there." God gives us many promises on which we can base that assurance. "For ye have not received the spirit of bondage again to fear; but ye have received the Spirit of adoption, whereby we cry, Abba, Father. The Spirit itself beareth witness with our spirit, that we are the children of God" (Romans 8:15, 16). "Ye were sealed with that holy Spirit of promise, which is the earnest of our inheritance until the redemption of the purchased possession,

---

[1]   Mary Ann Kidder, "Is My Name Written There?"

unto the praise of his glory" (Ephesians 1:13, 14). "Hereby know we that we dwell in him, and he in us, because he hath given us of his Spirit" (1 John 4:13).

Nice words, but how many of us skimmed over them hastily? We have heard them before. But let something happen—an illness, a death, a failure repented of—anything that jolts our assurance, and we read these words eagerly. Perhaps we should allow ourselves to be more comforted even on our pleasant days.

The comfort of spiritual health. A sick person may huddle in an armchair, wrap blankets around himself, and drink hot tea—only to shiver on. A healthy person runs out into the wind, buttons his jacket as he goes, and hardly even thinks about comfort; but he is more comfortable than a sick person. The comfort comes from deep within.

A spiritually ill person is miserable, even though he tries to soothe himself with excuses and reasonings. The Old Testament prophet said, "They have healed the hurt of the daughter of my people slightly, saying, Peace, peace; when there is no peace" (Jeremiah 8:11). But a spiritually healthy person does not have time to nurse his grievances and pity himself. He is busy serving the Lord.

The comfort of security against the powers of darkness. It was only after the Spirit of God departed from Saul that an evil spirit came to trouble him. As long as the Holy Spirit resides in us, we need not worry about such a disaster happening to us. "Greater is he that is in you, than he that is in the world" (1 John 4:4).

The comfort of a sense of direction. Sometimes we hear of a traveler lost in a snowy wilderness who comes upon someone's footprints and thinks, "Wonderful! I'll follow them." After some time he realizes with horror that he has been walking in a huge circle and following his own footprints. Suddenly he is absolutely alone again and hopelessly lost.

The Holy Spirit is to us what the traveler thought he was finding when he first saw tracks in the snow. Indeed He is better than that; He is a guide through the wilderness. He offers His chart, the Bible, and helps us to understand it. No wilderness is too wide or barren if we know we are heading in the right direction.

The comfort of His own loyalty. Even in the most painful or humiliating situations, He is there. We all hope never to become crippled or to experience a devastating illness. But if we ever do, one thought can comfort us: "Is my body good enough for the Holy Spirit to dwell in?" The answer is always yes if we love the Lord. And when our bodies finally do become too decrepit to contain life and our spirit moves out, He will go with us and take us to glory forever.

No wonder it was said of Jesus, "They shall call his name Emmanuel, which being interpreted is, God with us" (Matthew 1:23). That truth still stands every day of our lives. Always He is with us. He brightens all our days and gives us a North Star in our darkest nights.

> On land or sea, what matters where?
> Where Jesus is, 'tis heaven there.
> —*Charles Butler*

Index